The Microwave Cookbook

Carol Bowen is a freelance home economist and cookery writer. She has
contributed to the national press and magazines, broadcast on radio,
acted as consultant to manufacturers of food and kitchenware, done
photographic styling for advertising and books and worked as cookery
consultant for TV AM's *X-Cel Diet* with Diana Dors. She is married and
lives with her husband and young daughter in Surrey.

Other cookery books available in Pan

Carol Bowen

The
Microwave
Cookbook

Revised edition

Pan Original
Pan Books London and Sydney

First published 1979 by Pan Books Ltd,
Cavaye Place, London SW10 9PG
This revised edition published 1984
19 18 17 16 15 14 13 12 11 10
©Carol Bowen 1979, 1984

Illustrations (c) Kim Palmer 1984

ISBN 0 330 28644 7

Printed and bound in Great Britain by
Cox & Wyman Ltd, Reading

Contents

Acknowledgements I should like to offer my grateful thanks to Philips Electronics and Sharp Electronics (UK) Ltd for kindly supplying the microwave ovens on which all testing was done for this book.

Special thanks also go to Claire James and Caryll Fielder who typed and made sense of my drafted recipes and notes, to Jackie Goodwin for her double-checking and testing, and finally to my husband Peter for his constructive advice and sense of humour at all times!

Introduction

The introduction and development of the domestic microwave oven has made possible some of my wildest hopes and dreams. As an enthusiastic cook, busy journalist and recently, new mother, I like to cook extensively and creatively but generally in the minimum amount of time. The microwave oven enables me to do all of this – it has at times seemed quite magical. To be able to heat the baby's bottle to the perfect temperature in just thirty seconds at 4 o'clock in the morning makes the machine take on mystical qualities!

But a magic box it is not and I hope this book will go some way towards explaining how the microwave oven works and how you can get the very best from it.

The comprehensive microwave know-how section at the beginning of the book has recently been revised and will take you step by step through the mechanics of microwaves from their construction to their cooking action – giving advice and tips wherever applicable for getting the best results.

Included too is an extensive new recipe section – larger and more comprehensive than before – containing many new recipes, as well as some of the old time-honoured favourites from the earlier edition.

The final chapter in this book deals with the latest in microwave cooking – microwave with convection cooking – which offers a new dimension again to microwave cooking and will surely become a favourite for the future.

Which all adds up to what I hope is a more comprehensive and exciting view of the microwave. Bon appetit!

Carol Bowen

Microwave know-how

What is microwave energy?

Microwave energy is a type of high frequency radio wave positioned at the top end of the radio band. The waves are close together, but not as powerful as infra-red rays. They are in no way harmful and are far removed from x-rays, gamma rays and ultra violet rays which are known to damage human cells. Microwaves do not damage cells and, equally important, they are non-cumulative.

The mechanics of microwave cooking are very simple. Inside the microwave cooker, usually situated to the back right-hand corner of the oven, is the magnetron vacuum tube. This converts ordinary household electrical energy into high-frequency microwaves. These microwaves are passed, via the wave guide, into the wave stirrer fan, which distributes the microwaves evenly throughout the oven.

The microwaves can then do one of three things: (a) they can be reflected from a surface. Metals reflect microwaves, which is why they are safely contained within the oven cavity and why cooking utensils must be non-metallic; (b) they can pass through a substance. Glass, pottery, china, paper and most plastics allow them to pass through; (c) the microwaves can be absorbed by a substance. The microwaves are absorbed by the moisture molecules in food, causing them to vibrate rapidly, producing heat to cook the food. The moisture molecules vibrate many thousands of times per minute producing an intense heat which cooks the food – this accounts for the speed of microwave cooking.

However, since there is no applied surface heat, food does not brown readily on the outside with short cooking times. Browning will still take place, however, during long cooking times, e.g. when you are cooking a 5 kg (12 lb) turkey for say 1¾ hours.

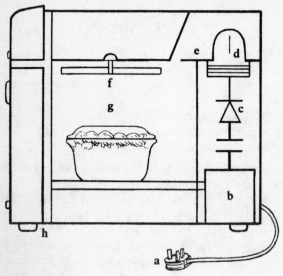

Cross-section of a microwave oven

The microwave oven

All ovens consist of a basic unit comprising a door, magnetron, wave guide, wave stirrer, power supply, power cord and controls. Some have additional features such as an automatic defrosting system, variable power control, browning element, turntable, or integral thermometer or temperature probe, but the basics upon which they work remains the same.

How the microwave oven works
(letters in bold refer to diagram opposite)

a The *plug* is inserted into the socket and the electricity flows to
b the *power transformer* which increases the ordinary household voltage. This passes into
c a *high-voltage rectifier and capacitor* which changes the high alternating voltage to indirectional voltage. The indirectional voltage is applied to
d the *magnetron* which converts the electrical energy into electromagnetic or microwave energy. This energy is then passed through to
e the *wave guide* which directs the microwave energy into the oven cavity. As the microwaves enter the oven
f the *wave stirrer* turns slowly to distribute the microwaves in an even pattern around the oven.
g The *oven cavity* made of metal contains the microwaves safely and deflects the waves from the walls and base of the oven to be absorbed by the food.
h The *oven door* and the door frame are filled with special seals to ensure that the microwaves are kept safely within the oven. Usually at least one cut-out device is incorporated so that the microwave energy is automatically switched off when the door is open.

The features on microwave ovens are numerous and each is worth examining. Study each feature and choose a model to suit your individual needs and requirements.

Controls

The very simplest controls on a microwave oven are likely to be a timer and a 'cook' button or switch. To operate, simply place the food in the oven cavity, close the door, set the timer for the cooking time required and start the microwave energy by depressing the 'cook' control. The microwave will cook with microwave energy until the timer moves to the off position when it will automatically stop the microwave energy.

Exactly the same would happen if the door were opened during the cooking period. Restarting can take place only when the door is closed and the 'cook' button depressed again.

Timer control Most microwave ovens have at least one timer – and generally they are for up to 30 minutes. Graduations of a second are usually incorporated at the lower end of the scale for short cooking times where timing is very critical, whereas half-minute – and sometimes minute – graduations are given at the higher end of the scale. Often the control is in the form of a sliding device, not just as a dial, and care should be taken to set the timer accurately.

Cook control Sometimes called the start control since it simply switches on the microwave power whether you are thawing, reheating or prime cooking.

On/off control As well as alerting the cooking operation, this control often switches on the cooling fan and brings on the interior oven light. On some ovens there is a very short delay operation, lasting about 10 seconds after switching on, to allow the power source to warm up prior to use. If your oven does not have an on/off control it will be operated automatically when the oven is switched on at the power supply.

Power level control Discussed in greater detail later, but very simply this means you can choose to decrease the microwave energy, introducing a 'slower' cooking rate for items that require slower cooking. Basic microwaves with on/off controls operate the power on a constant full or high power, variable control microwave ovens have a control that enables the power to be reduced to low, medium or high, or graduated in numbers from say 1–6, or expressed verbally as simmer, roast, reheat, etc.

Indicator lights These are very useful as a reminder that a cooking operation has been set, is in progress or has finished.

Audible reminders Usually in the form of a bell or buzzer, they will remind you that a cooking operation is complete.

Cooking guide A panel is sometimes incorporated into the front of the oven giving basic cooking information and times needed for various cooking operations.

Thermometers These may only be used if the manufacturer specifically states that it is possible. Some manufacturers supply integral thermometers specially designed for use in ovens and in conjunction with a control for cooking meats and roasts.

Turntable Some ovens incorporate a turntable instead of, or as an extra to, the wave stirrer; its purpose is to distribute the microwaves evenly through the food. The revolving turntable can often be removed but if not this may restrict the size and shape of dishes that can be used in that microwave.

'Off' indicator Indicates when cooking time is complete. It may or may not turn off the oven light.

Interior oven light This generally lights up as soon as the appliance is turned on. Some models have a separate switch and one model has the light incorporated with the 'cook' control.

Splash guard Sometimes the wave stirrer has a special protective guard to protect it from food splashing. Remove and clean it according to manufacturer's instructions.

Removable floor or base Made of special glass or plastic, it acts as a spillage plate and positions the food to best advantage in the oven.

Door latch Some doors have no latch at all and have an up-and-over operation. Others have a door latch or a push button incorporated in the door handle.

Additional features

Automatic defrost Defrosting can take place in the microwave oven by giving the food a short burst of energy followed by a rest period and then repeating the process until the food is evenly thawed.

An automatic defrost button will take care of this procedure for you by automatically turning the energy on and off at regular intervals. A very useful extra for freezer owners.

Browning element A browning element, somewhat like an electric grill, is sometimes incorporated into the top of the microwave oven and can be used to pre-brown food or brown it after being cooked in the microwave or during microwave cooking.

Slow cook control A control which enables the microwave output to be reduced or the power to be 'pulsed', therefore slowing down the cooking time.

Keep warm/stay hot control This control, based on a very low power pulse, enables food to be kept warm for up to one hour without continuing the cooking process.

Two power-level cooking The very latest revolutionary design for micro-wave ovens. In this type of oven the microwaves enter from the sides rather than from the top of the oven. This means two cooking levels or more may be employed simultaneously with different power ratings.

Types of microwave ovens

Portable Most microwave ovens available to date are of the portable kind, simply requiring a 13- or 15-amp plug. They sit neatly on a work surface or trolley, and are light enough to move from room to room or out into the garden on an extension lead for garden parties.

Double oven There are a few microwave ovens on the market which are incorporated into conventional ovens. The microwave acts as a second oven, separate from the conventional oven.

Combination cookers These have the facility to cook conventionally or by microwave energy in one oven. The oven itself combines the efficiency of the microwave with the benefits of conventional heat. The user can use conventional heat or microwave energy separately or both together. A further choice is also possible if the oven is fan-assisted.

Checklist for microwave cooking

Starting temperature of food The higher the starting temperature, the faster the food will be heated or cooked. For frozen foods use the microwave as a defroster first and then as a cooking medium.

Density of food The denser the food, the longer it will take to cook. A fairly small but dense piece of steak may be similar in size to a hamburger but the looser nature of the hamburger means it will cook faster in the microwave.

When heating a fairly deep, dense mass of food such as a pie, the centre of the pie will always be the coolest and most difficult to heat; make a well and insert a rolled-up 2.5cm (1 in) piece of brown paper in the centre to encourage the transmission of microwaves to the centre. Alternatively use a ring mould for this purpose.

Shape of food Irregular shapes should be avoided, e.g. a leg of lamb which is thick at the thigh end but thin at the shin. If cooked in the microwave as it stands the shin part is likely to be over-cooked. Bone, roll and tie the leg to form a uniform shape and the meat will cook much more satisfactorily.

Where unstuffed chickens and turkeys are concerned, the wings and legs should be tucked into the body shape of the bird to avoid overheating and dehydration in these areas. They may also be wrapped in lightweight aluminium foil which can be removed during the last 10 minutes of cooking, but be sure the foil does not touch the sides of the oven.

Timing and quantities The actual operation of a microwave oven is simple, but judging how long food takes to cook requires some trial and error. Each brand of oven has its own cooking guide giving approximate timings for foods. One feature often overlooked, however, is that the cooking time increases with the amount of food or the number of separate items in the oven.

Additional portions call for increased times. Unlike in a conventional oven, where six potatoes may cook in one hour, in the microwave oven one potato may take 8 minutes, two 15 minutes, three 22 minutes, etc. Generally work on a few minutes less than doubling the original time for each item added to the oven.

Experimenting with your oven will give you accurate times, but always remember it is best to undercook.

For each microwave oven there is an ideal load at which the oven gives its most impressive performance and at which it compares favourably with the conventional oven. Trial and error will help you find this if it is not specified in the instruction manual.

Browning The brown surface colour of foods is due to a chemical reaction between food sugars and amino acids. This reaction proceeds slowly at low temperatures and is accelerated at higher temperatures. In microwave cooking, the surface temperature of foods does not change over quick cooking times. Because of this most foods cooked in the microwave oven lack the browning expected of them.

Aids to browning meat and poultry

- Brown before or after cooking under a preheated conventional grill.
- Pre-brown using a special microwave browning dish.
- Use a special commercial browning agent or mix specially produced to coat meat, fish or poultry prior to microwave cooking.
- Use a home-made browning agent to coat or brush food prior to cooking. For example, coat with browned breadcrumbs, dust with ground paprika, coat with a colourful dry soup mix, brush with tomato sauce, barbecue sauce, brown sauce or soy sauce, or coat with crushed crisps.

Aids to browning cakes, biscuits and breads

- Sprinkle cakes and biscuits with chopped nuts, spices, chopped glacé fruits, toasted coconut or chocolate vermicelli before cooking.
- Frost or ice cakes, biscuits and breads after cooking to camouflage the pale crust.
- Quickly brown breads under a preheated hot grill after microwave cooking.
- Sprinkle bread with herbs, poppyseeds, cracked wheat, buckwheat, grated cheese, toasted sesame seeds or chopped nuts prior to cooking.

Composition of food Fats and sugars absorb microwave energy at a greater rate than other foods and therefore cook faster. Foods with a low moisture content also tend to cook faster than wetter mixtures of the same shape, density and size.

Size of the food Larger pieces of food take longer to cook than smaller pieces because microwaves only penetrate to a depth of about 5cm

(2in). For best results and even cooking make sure pieces of food are of a uniform size.

Standing time All food continues to cook for a little while after it has been removed from the oven, whether cooked by microwave or conventional method, due to the residual heat still within the food. With microwave cooking it is important to observe this standing time and therefore to undercook the food a little to account for it. All the recipes in this book do this, so you need not observe this point when following the recipes given, only when trying out new recipes. Standing time is usually accounted for at the end of the cooking time but in some cases it may take place during the cooking time, e.g. when meat is being roasted and is allowed to rest during the cooking procedure. Standing time should, however, be allowed at the end of the cooking time on such occasions, too.

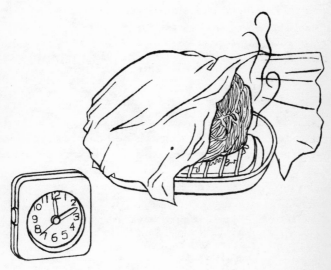

Wrap joints of meat loosely in foil while leaving them to rest after roasting in the oven, to complete the cooking process

Bones in meat Generally food next to the bone will cook faster than the remaining meat because bone conducts heat into food. For this reason it is recommended that meats should be boned and rolled into a

9

uniform shape for microwave cooking. If boning is not possible then shield the area next to the bone with a small piece of foil to prevent over-cooking. Place the foil on the area about half-way through the cooking time.

Vulnerable foods Those foods which attract microwave energy, like cheese with its high fat content or meat with integral bones, are best buried or protected in a less vulnerable food like a sauce, or covered with vegetables during cooking.

Height in oven Just like in conventional cooking, those areas nearest to the energy source will also cook faster in microwave cooking. This may be near the top or base of your oven depending upon model and manufacturer. For even results, turn over, rotate, re-arrange, or shield vulnerable areas to even out this irregularity.

Microwave cooking techniques

Turning foods over

This is something that we practise every day in conventional cooking to ensure food cooks evenly. The same practice must also be observed in microwave cooking. In most cases, turn the food over half-way through the cooking time unless the recipe instructions specify more regular turning. A fork, a pair of tongs or spatula will help in doing this.

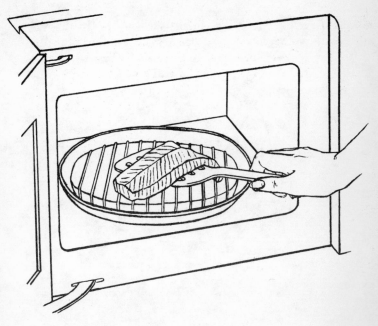

Turn food over half-way through the cooking time

Stirring foods

Because microwaves only penetrate foods to a depth of 5cm (2in), stirring is necessary to distribute the heat evenly in microwave cooking. Always stir from the outside of the dish to the centre. The outer edges will always cook or heat faster than the centre, which receives less microwave energy. A wooden spoon or spatula is useful in doing this and for short cooking periods it may be left in the microwave during cooking.

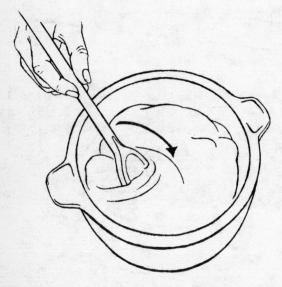

Stir foods once or more during microwave cooking to distribute the heat evenly

Rotating foods or dishes

When a food cannot be stirred or turned over, it is most important to rotate the food or dish to ensure even cooking. In most cases a quarter- or half-turn half-way through the cooking time is all that is needed. This need not be done with microwave ovens which have a turntable.

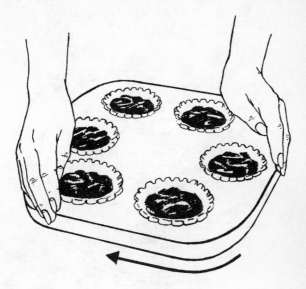

Rotate baking dishes so that the food cooks evenly

Re-arranging foods

Another way of ensuring that food cooks, reheats or defrosts evenly is to re-arrange the food during cooking. No microwave has a perfectly tuned energy pattern and most microwave owners will experience hot or cool spots in their ovens – re-arranging foods during the cooking time overcomes the problem of such 'blackspot' areas and ensures even results.

To ensure even cooking, rearrange food part-way through the cooking time

Covering foods

If you cover food during microwave cooking you effectively speed up the cooking time, hold in the moisture, and also prevent spattering on the oven walls, therefore saving yourself from unnecessary cleaning.

There are several ways in which you can effectively cover foods during microwave cooking. A tight-fitting lid to a dish is probably the most obvious; if you are using a dish without a lid try placing a saucer over the dish. Plastic cook-in bags or roaster bags also make good coverage, especially for cooking vegetables and roasts. Remember to replace any metal ties with rubber bands or string. Absorbent kitchen towel is another useful cover, especially in covering fatty foods like bacon or those with a lot of moisture like jacket potatoes. If the dish is of an unusual shape, or if the food protrudes above the dish in an irregular way, then greaseproof paper or cling film will prove useful covers since they readily mould to the contents. Secure any greaseproof paper around the dish with string or tuck under the base.

Cover food with a tight-fitting lid or with cling film to speed up cooking, or use a roasting bag. Prick the film or bag with a knife before cooking

Removing excess cooking juices

Any juices that are produced during microwave cooking will continue to attract microwave energy and can, in effect, slow down the cooking process. Remove any juices with a bulb baster at regular intervals during the cooking time. If the food starts to dry out towards the latter stages of the cooking time, these juices can always be re-introduced.

Remove cooking juices with a bulb baster

Drying techniques

In many ways the microwave simulates a steam cabinet and does not produce crisp or dry results. Absorbent kitchen towel is one of the most useful materials that you can use to overcome this. Place jacket potatoes on a double-thickness of absorbent kitchen towel and they will cook dry and crisp. Bacon if covered with or placed between two sheets of absorbent kitchen towel will also cook dry and crisp rather than greasy or soggy. The same technique can also be used to dry herbs or flowers in the microwave. Place the chosen herbs or flowers between two pieces of absorbent kitchen towel and cook until they are dry enough to crumble.

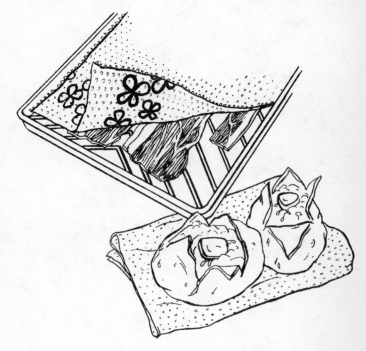

Use kitchen paper to absorb steam in the microwave and to produce crisp results with bacon or jacket potatoes

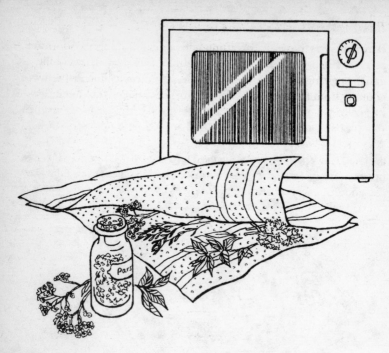

Dry herbs by cooking fresh herbs between sheets of absorbent kitchen paper

Releasing pressure in foods

Any foods that have a tight-fitting skin or membrane must be pricked prior to cooking in the microwave. Failure to do so will inevitably cause bursting or exploding as the pressure mounts during the cooking from the production of steam. The same procedure must be observed when using cook-in bags, boil-in-the-bag pouches, and roaster bags. Always pierce cling film in a couple of places if using as a cover for a dish.

This technique must also be used when cooking whole eggs – microwave energy is attracted to the fats in the egg yolk and therefore the yolk cooks faster than the white. Prick the yolk carefully with a cocktail stick or the tip of a knife to ensure that the yolk does not explode.

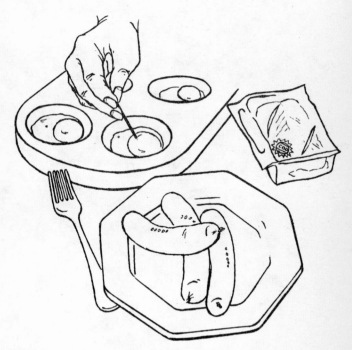

Prick the membrane of egg yolks and the skin of sausages carefully with a cocktail stick before cooking to prevent them from exploding

Shielding foods

Shielding is a technique employed to protect vulnerable parts of a food from over-cooking. The sensitive areas that are prone to over-cooking include the breasts, wing tips, drumsticks and tail-end of poultry, the heads and tails of fish, the thinner end of a leg of lamb, the inside edge of a pastry flan and any fatty areas of food, like the fatty rind of a piece of bacon, pork or ham. To shield these areas from microwave energy it is recommended that small strips of foil are used to cover the sensitive parts. This is the only time when small pieces of foil are generally permissible within the microwave oven. Wrap the foil around the affected part or secure to the food with cocktail sticks. Add the foil either prior to cooking and remove half-way through the cooking time, or as the areas seem to be just cooked.

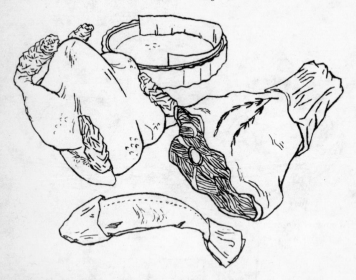

Shield the thin, vulnerable parts of food from burning in the oven by wrapping them in small pieces of aluminium foil

Arranging foods in the microwave

In just the same way as we arrange food for even cooking in the conventional oven or under the conventional grill, we must arrange food carefully in the microwave oven to achieve even cooking. If you are cooking several items of the same food then arrange these in a ring pattern on the base of the oven or in a dish. A ring pattern is recommended because the centre of a dish receives less energy than the edges.

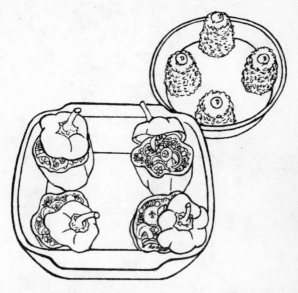

Arrange regular shaped foods in a ring pattern in the dish, near the edge of the dish where they will receive most energy

Any irregular-shaped foods like chicken drumsticks, broccoli, chops, or whole fish should also be positioned to take this action into account. Always make sure that the foods are positioned so that the thicker meatier parts are at the edge of the dish, where they will receive most energy, and that the thinner portions are pointing to the centre, where they will receive less.

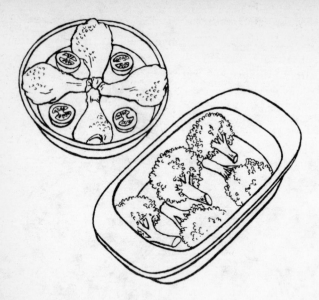

Always arrange food in the dish so that the thicker parts are near the edge of the dish where they receive most microwave energy

Since some foods are more vulnerable to cooking by microwave, we must also arrange them in such a way to make best use of the energy. Bury these foods – which include cheese and meat – deep in the dish; or cover them with a sauce so that they do not over-cook while the remaining ingredients stay undercooked or even raw.

Pros and cons of microwave cooking

Advantages
Speed You can save up to 75 per cent of normal cooking time.

Economy Since it is used for shorter cooking times you can save up to 50 per cent of your electricity or cooking-fuel bills.

Efficiency Energy is directed straight to the food and there is no energy loss to oven cavity or kitchen. It is up to four times as efficient as cooking conventionally. No costly warm up periods are required.

Smells Cooking odours tend to be largely contained within the oven and do not spread throughout the house.

Coolness Because of the mechanics of microwave cooking, the oven, dishes and kitchen all tend to stay cool – only the food is piping hot. Often oven gloves are not required and there is less chance of a nasty burn.

Defrosting A special bonus to freezer owners – no need to remember to take the food out of the freezer in the morning for the evening meal. Meals can be more spontaneous and menu-planning becomes easier.

Cleanliness Foods do not bake on the oven walls so all that is required is a wipe with a damp soapy cloth. Your kitchen will stay cleaner and less greasy, too.

Washing up There is less of this if you cook in the same dish as you would usually serve in at the table. Washing up is easier as the food is not baked on to cooking utensil surfaces for such long periods.

Combination cooking Even those dishes you prefer cooked conventionally can usually be speeded up by prior or post cooking in the microwave; this leaves you more time to spend with your family and friends.

Reheating No more curled up dinners. The microwave enables you to cook meals, plate them and reheat them as if fresh should your family eat at different times of the day. Frozen plated meals can also be reheated in minutes without drying out.

Bulk cooking When the opportunity arises you can set a whole day aside for bulk microwave cooking for the freezer. The dishes can then be defrosted and reheated in the microwave as required.

Nutritional value Because of the precise timing required for microwave cooking, there is less risk of over-cooking foods, and so flavour, colour and texture are kept at their best and less nutritional value is lost.

Shrinkage Cooked according to instructions, foods tend to shrink less.

Over-cooking This becomes a thing of the past if you set the timer correctly and wait for the audible timer warning.

Disadvantages

Browning Since there is no applied surface heat, food does not brown readily in the microwave with short cooking times. See page 81 for some helpful hints.

Metals These cannot be used in the microwave oven.

You cannot cook . . . Yorkshire puddings (they go flat), meringues, scones, or some rich cakes made by the creaming method, and pancakes. Some of these dishes can, however, be reheated satisfactorily in the microwave.

Dishes and utensils

Without doubt, the range of cooking utensils that can be used in the microwave oven is wider than those used for cooking conventionally. Serving dishes, glass, china, pottery, paper and some plastics that could not be used in the conventional oven now find a place in the microwave.

A few exceptions do, however, exist. Most manufacturers object to the use of metal. Even small amounts present in the oven will reflect the microwaves so that they do not penetrate the food to be cooked. Therefore, avoid metal dishes, baking trays and metal baking tins, foil dishes, cast-iron casseroles, plates and china trimmed with a metallic design, any dish with a metal screw or attachment and paper-coated metal ties often found with freezer and cook bags.

Most manufacturers agree that it is permissible to use aluminium foil for protecting those portions of food that tend to cook more quickly than others. Use thin foil to protect the wings of poultry from over-cooking, the centre of a roast slice of meat from becoming too well done and the edge of a casserole from over-cooking. Do take care, however, to make sure the foil does not touch the edge of the oven.

Glass, pottery and china Oven-proof and plain glass, pottery and china are all suitable for use in the microwave oven. Be sure to check that they do not have any metallic trim, screws or handles, and if using a pottery dish that it is non-porous.

Paper For low heat and short cooking times, such as thawing, reheating or very short prime cooking, and for foods with a low fat, sugar or water content, paper is a good utensil for microwave oven use. Napkins, paper towels, cups, cartons, paper freeze wrap and paper pulp board often used for meat packaging are all suitable. Paper towels are especially useful for cooking fatty foods since they absorb excess fats and oils and can be used to prevent splattering on the walls of the oven.

Wax-coated paper cups and plates should be avoided since the high temperature of the food will cause the wax to melt; they can, however, be used for defrosting cold items like frozen cakes and desserts.

Plastics 'Dishwasher Safe' is a useful indicator as to whether or not a plastic is suitable in the microwave. Plastic dishes and containers, unless made of a thermoplastic material, should not be used for cooking food with a high fat or sugar content, since the heat of the food may be too much for the plastic and may cause it to melt or lose its shape.

Plastic film and devices like boil-in-the-bags work well in the microwave. Pierce the film or bag before cooking to allow the steam to escape, and take care when removing the plastic film in case there is any steam remaining.

Do not attempt to cook in thin plastic storage bags as they will not withstand the heat of the food. Thicker storage bags are acceptable. Use elastic bands, string or non-metal ties to secure the bags loosely before cooking.

Melamine is not recommended for microwave cooking since it absorbs enough microwave energy to cause charring.

Cotton and linen Napkins can be used for short reheating purposes, e.g. reheating bread rolls, but check that the material is 100 per cent cotton or linen and does not contain any synthetic fibres.

Wooden bowls and basketware These are only suitable for short reheating purposes, otherwise the wood or wicker will tend to char, dry out or crack.

Roasting bags A very clean, convenient way of cooking many foods. This is particularly true of meats, since browning takes place more readily within them than in other plastic bags. However, the metal ties must be replaced with elastic bands or string. Snip a couple of holes in the bag to aid the escape of steam.

Microwave containers With the increased popularity of microwave cooking comes a host of special innovations in microwave cookware. Several ranges manufactured from polythene, polystyrene and thermoplastic are now widely available and come in a comprehensive range of shapes and sizes.

Thermometers Ones made specially for microwave ovens are available but can be used in an oven only when specified by that oven's manufacturer. To take the temperature reading with a standard meat thermometer, remove the food from the oven, insert the thermometer, into the thickest portion of food and let it stand for about 10 minutes to register the internal temperature. If more cooking is needed, remove the thermometer and return the meat to the oven.

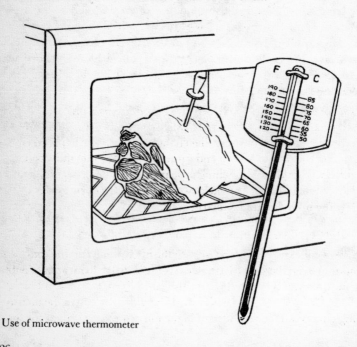

Use of microwave thermometer

Some newer ovens have an automatic cooking control, a temperature sensing probe, that can be inserted into a roast or other food while in the oven. When the food reaches a preset temperature, the oven turns itself off automatically.

Browning dishes Available from most microwave dealers, these duplicate the conventional browning and searing processes of conventional cooking. Especially useful for pre-browning meat, poultry and fish, they can also be used for 'frying' eggs and sandwiches, and browning vegetables.

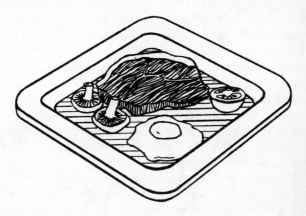

Browning dishes will sear food before it is cooked in the microwave oven

The browning dish, made of a glass-ceramic substance with a special coating that absorbs microwave energy, is preheated in the microwave until the base coating changes colour. The food is then placed on the dish to brown and turned to sear the remaining sides. Preheating times and browning or searing times differ according to the food being cooked and the power output of the oven. Always follow the manufacturer's instructions.

Remember

If you are going to cook food in both the microwave and the conventional oven, be sure to use an oven-proof dish. If you are in doubt about the suitability of a dish, try this simple test:
Fill a heatproof glass cup with water and place the cup in the utensil being checked. Place the utensil in the microwave oven and cook for

1¼ minutes. If the water is warm in the cup and the utensil is cool, go ahead and use the utensil. If the utensil if warm or even hot and the water is still cool or barely lukewarm, do not use it for microwave cooking.

The shape of dish to use

After checking the material of the dish or utensil, consider its shape, too. Ideally, the more regular the shape the better it is suited to microwave cooking, e.g. a round shape is better than an oval, as quicker cooking may take place at the 'ends' of the oval resulting in an unevenly cooked product. A straight-sided container is better than a curved one, as the microwaves can penetrate more evenly. A large shallow dish is better than a small deep one as the food offers a greater surface area to microwaves.

Oven control settings

The simplest form of microwave oven has an on/off control whereby energy is either switched on or off. The energy that is turned on operates on full power.

A certain amount of control over energy has now been made possible with variable or multiple control ovens. The variable control dial 'pulses' the energy into the microwave cavity thereby allowing different speeds of microwave cooking. The pulse control turns the microwave power on and off automatically every so many seconds (see guide, below). This way the food receives a quick burst of energy with rests in between to enable the heat to distribute itself evenly. This is especially useful when defrosting foods and cooking dishes that need slower cooking, e.g. less tender cuts of meat and delicate dishes like egg custards.

This control gives the cook a greater amount of flexibility in cooking operations, allowing her to keep food warm, defrost foods, simmer, roast and reheat foods as well as prime cooking foods on full power.

Use of power control dial

Low (1, keep warm, low or 2) Energy on for about 25 per cent of the time.

Use for keeping foods warm for up to half an hour, softening butter, cream cheese and chocolate, proving yeast mixtures, and very gentle cooking.

Defrost (3, stew, medium/low or 4) Energy on for about 40 per cent of the time. Use for defrosting meat, poultry and fish, finishing off slow-cooking casseroles and stews. Use for cooking delicate egg dishes and less tender cuts of meat.

Medium (4, defrost, medium or 5) Energy on for about 50 per cent of the time. Use for roasting meats and poultry, cooking fish, yeast doughs, pâtés, rice and pasta.

Medium/high (6, roast, medium/high or 7–8) Energy on for 60 to 75 per cent of the time. Use for quick reheating of individual meals frozen on plates and frozen dishes once defrosted.

Full (7, full/high or 10) Energy on 100 per cent of the time. The only setting on basic on/off models. Use for most prime cooking, quick reheating of shallow dishes of food and fast-speed dishes.

Note: It is important to use the power control settings above in relation to the chart given on page 30 which shows comparable descriptions of variable control power settings for popular microwave ovens and gives a guide to adjusting the cooking time.

Guide to comparative temperature settings

Description of settings used in this book	**low**		**defrost**	**medium**		**medium/ high**	**full**
Description of settings available on popular microwave ovens	1 keep warm low 2	2 simmer 3	3 stew medium/low 4	4 defrost medium 5	5 bake medium 6	6 roast high 7–8	7 full/high normal 10
Approximate % power input	25%	30%	40%	50%	60%	75%	100%
Approximate power output in watts	150w	200w	250w	300w	400w	500–550w	650–700w
Cooking time in minutes	4	3¼	2½	2	1¾	1¼	1
	8	6¾	5	4	3¼	2¾	2
	12	10	7½	6	5	4	3
	16	13¼	10	8	6¾	5¼	4
	20	16¾	12½	10	8¼	6¾	5
	24	20	15	12	10	8	6
	28	23¼	17½	14	11¾	9¼	7
	32	26¾	20	16	13¼	10¾	8
	36	30	22½	18	15	12	9
	40	33¼	25	20	16½	13¼	10

* For times greater than 10 minutes simply add the figures in the appropriate columns together.

Siting the microwave oven

The microwave oven is a most versatile cooking machine since it is portable. Providing that you have a steady and secure surface, a suitable fused power socket, and sufficient ventilation, then you can site your microwave almost anywhere. Kitchen work surfaces are favourite locations but you could just as easily place your microwave on a secure trolley, in a dining room, or even outside on the patio to help with the demands of alfresco entertaining.

Most microwaves can be taken away on holiday to caravans and holiday homes – remember, however, to have your microwave serviced regularly in case bumps or jolts have loosened any mechanisms.

Many microwaves can now be permanently installed into fitted kitchens with special housing units for a totally integrated appearance. If you intend to make such a housing yourself then do follow the manufacturer's guidelines on venting space required above and around the unit.

Cleaning the microwave oven

The microwave oven must be one of the simplest cooking mediums to keep clean since food does not burn, stick or char on to the sides of the oven. Since the oven walls stay relatively cool all that is required is a wipe with a damp cloth and a little detergent from time to time. Remember to wipe up any splashes or spills as they occur, however – if you don't they will continue to absorb microwave energy as the oven is used thereby reducing the speed of cooking.

It is sometimes necessary with heavy use to deodorize the oven – this can be done by placing a bowl containing three parts water to one part lemon juice in the oven and cooking on full power for 5–10 minutes. Then wipe with a dry cloth.

Some ovens also have a removable and disposable filter – check in your microwave handbook. If it has then remember to change and replace it according to the manufacturer's advice.

Guide to recipes

Since microwave cooking is so very different from the conventional
way of cooking it is important to read the introductory section in this
book first.

All the recipes in this book were created and tested using
microwave ovens with a power output of 700 watts on full power. The
ovens also had variable power ranging from 150–700 watts for greater
flexibility (see the chart on page 30 for temperature and cooking
settings). It is important to remember that if your microwave has a
power output higher than 700 watts to reduce the cooking time
accordingly and if your microwave has a power output lower than 700
watts to increase the cooking time accordingly. A few simple trial and
error cooking tests will tell you how much to adjust the recipe times by
should this be the case.

Metric measurements

Metric measurements may vary from one recipe to another within
this book and it is essential to follow either metric or imperial
measures. The recipes have been specially balanced to get the very
best results whether using metric or Imperial measures so it is
important not to interchange quantities.

Defrosting chart

Food	Quantity	Power setting	Time in minutes	Instructions
Meat				
Bacon	1 225g/8oz pkt	defrost	2–3	Turn over half-way through cooking.
	1 450g/1lb joint	defrost	8	Allow to stand 20–30 minutes.
Burgers	2 100g/4 oz	defrost	2–3	Allow to stand 2 minutes.
	4 100g/4oz	defrost	5	Allow to stand 5 minutes.
Casserole with vegetables	4 portions	full	14–16	To thaw *and reheat*.
Sausages	450g/1lb thick	defrost	5–6	Turn and re-arrange half-way through cooking. Stand 5 minutes.
	450g/1lb thin	defrost	5	
Shepherd's pie	400g/14oz	full	5	Allow to stand 2 minutes then cook a further 6 minutes. To thaw *and reheat*.
Roast meat with gravy	350g/12oz	full	3	Allow to stand 3 minutes then cook a further 3½ minutes. To thaw *and reheat*.

Food	Quantity	Power setting	Time in minutes	Instructions
Fish				
Cod in sauce	2 boil in bags	full	12–13	Pierce bag and turn once or
	4 boil in bags	full	16–17	twice during cooking. To thaw *and cook*.
Smoked haddock	1 175g/6oz cook in bag	full	6	Pierce bag and turn once during cooking. To thaw *and cook*.
Buttered kipper fillets	1 175g/6oz cook in bag	full	6	Pierce bag and turn once during cooking. To thaw *and cook*.
Fish cakes	2 50g/2oz	full	2½	Allow to stand 3 minutes then cook a further 1 minute.
Soups	300ml/½ pint	full	3	Break down solid block during
	600ml/1 pint	full	6	cooking.
Bread	1 large unsliced loaf	defrost	6–8	Allow to stand 5–10 minutes. Turn twice.
	1 small unsliced loaf	defrost	6	Allow to stand 10 minutes. Turn twice.
	1 large sliced loaf	defrost	10–12	Allow to stand 10–15 minutes. Turn several times.
	1 slice	defrost	½–1	Check constantly.
	2 rolls	defrost	½–1	Allow to stand 2–3 minutes.
	4 rolls	defrost	1½–3	Stand on paper towel.
	2 pitta breads	defrost	1½–2	Stand on paper towel.
	2 croissants	defrost	½–1	Stand on paper towel.
	2 crumpets	full	½–¾	Stand on paper towel. To thaw

Food	Quantity	Power setting	Time in minutes	Instructions
	2 teacakes	full	¾–1	and reheat. Stand on paper towel. To thaw and reheat.
Cakes & biscuits				
Biscuits	225g/8oz	defrost	1	Turn once and allow to stand 5 minutes.
Small light fruit cake	1	defrost	5	Turn once. Allow to stand 10 minutes.
Buns/rock cakes	2	defrost	1–1½	Allow to stand 5 minutes.
Cream-filled sponge	1 15cm/6in cake	full	¾	Allow to stand 10–15 minutes.
Jam sponge	1 17.5cm/7 in cake	defrost	3	Allow to stand 5 minutes.
Cheesecake –fruit topped	family size	defrost	5–6	Turn twice.
	individual	defrost	1–1½	Allow to stand 5 minutes.
Doughnuts				
– jam	2	defrost	1½–2	Allow to stand 3 minutes.
– cream	2	defrost	1–1½	Allow to stand 3 minutes.
Eclairs	2	defrost	¾–1	Allow to stand 5–10 minutes.
Gateaux				
– black forest	1 15cm/6in	defrost	4–6	Allow to stand 30 minutes.
Scones	2	defrost	1–1½	Stand on paper towel.

Food	Quantity	Power setting	Time in minutes	Instructions
Rice and pasta				
Kedgeree	225g/8oz	full	5–6	Stir twice. To thaw *and reheat.*
Pasta (cooked)	275g/10oz	defrost	10	Stir twice. To thaw *and reheat.*
Rice (cooked)	225g/8oz	full	5–6	Stir twice. To thaw *and reheat.*
Sauces	300ml/½ pint	full	5–6	Stir twice. Whisk. To thaw *and reheat.*
Stock	300ml/½ pint	full	2½–3	Break down frozen block during cooking.
Miscellaneous				
Butter	250g/9oz block	defrost	2–3	Turn once and allow to stand 5 minutes.
Eggs				
– whites only	2	defrost	1½–2	Allow to stand 5 minutes.
Flans				
– unfilled, cooked pastry case in	1 17.5cm/7	defrost	1–1½	Allow to stand 3 minutes.
– filled flan	family size	full	4–5	Turn once. Allow to stand for 3 minutes. To thaw *and reheat.* Remove metal lid.
Fruit juice	1 178ml/6fl oz concentrate	full	1	

Food	Quantity	Power setting	Time in minutes	Instructions
Pancakes	8 stacked	defrost	6	Re-arrange twice. Allow to stand 5 minutes.
	4 stuffed	full	10	Turn twice. To thaw *and reheat*.
Pâté	1 198g/7oz pack	defrost	3–4	Allow to stand 15 minutes.
Pizza	individual	full	1½–2	Stand on paper towel. To thaw *and reheat*.
	family	full	3–4	Stand on paper towel. To thaw *and reheat*.
Yoghurt	1 small carton	full	1	Remove lid. Stir for 1 minute after cooking to mix.

Soups, starters and appetizers

French onion soup

Serves: 4
Power setting: full
Total cooking time: 15 minutes

50g/2oz butter
675g/1½lb onions, peeled and thinly sliced
1 tablespoon flour
900ml/1½pints boiling rich beef stock
salt and freshly ground black pepper
4 slices French bread, toasted
50g/2oz Gruyère cheese, grated

Place the butter in a large serving dish and cook for 1 minute to melt.
Add the onions and cook for a further 5 minutes or until softened. Stir
in the flour and cook for a further 2 minutes. Gradually add the stock,
blending well. Season to taste with salt and pepper and cook for 5
minutes, stirring half-way through the cooking time.

Sprinkle the toasted French bread with the cheese and float on top
of the prepared soup. Cook until the cheese melts, about 2 minutes.
Serve at once.

Vichyssoise

Serves: 4
Power setting: full
Total cooking time: 14 minutes

25g/1oz butter
450g/1lb leeks, washed and sliced
1 onion, peeled and sliced
2 large potatoes, peeled and chopped
450ml/¾ pint chicken stock
salt and freshly ground white pepper
300ml/½ pint milk
300ml/½pint double cream
snipped chives to garnish

Place the butter, leeks, onion and potatoes in a large dish. Cover and
cook for 7 minutes, stirring half-way through the cooking time. Add

the stock and salt and pepper to taste. Cover and cook for a further 5 minutes. Purée until smooth in a blender or pass through a fine sieve.

Stir in the milk and cream, cover and cook for a further 2 minutes. Allow to cool then chill thoroughly.

Serve chilled, sprinkled with snipped chives.

Microwave minestrone

Serves: 6–8
Power setting: full
Total cooking time: 41 minutes

225g/8oz salted belly pork, cut into 2.5cm/1in cubes
1 onion, peeled and finely chopped
2 cloves garlic, peeled and crushed
2 stalks celery, thinly sliced
2 carrots, peeled and sliced
2 tomatoes, peeled, seeded and chopped
150g/5oz macaroni
2.25l/4 pints beef stock
salt and freshly ground black pepper
100g/4oz frozen peas
100g/4 oz frozen green beans
To garnish:
chopped parsley
grated Parmesan cheese

Preheat a browning dish for 5 minutes, or according to the manufacturer's instructions. Add the pork turning quickly on all sides to brown evenly. Cook for 3 minutes.

Add the onion and garlic and cook for a further 3 minutes. Transfer to a large casserole dish and add the celery, carrots, tomatoes and macaroni. Pour in the beef stock, cover and cook for 25 minutes.

Season to taste with salt and pepper and stir in the peas and beans. Cover and cook for a further 5 minutes.

Serve hot, sprinkled with chopped parsley and Parmesan cheese.

Tangy tomato soup

Serves: 2
Power setting: full
Total cooking time: 11 minutes

25g/1oz butter
1 onion, peeled and finely chopped
1 teaspoon mustard powder
1 396g/14 oz can peeled tomatoes
150ml/¼ pint chicken stock
4 tablespoons orange juice
salt and freshly ground black pepper
To garnish:
chopped parsley
bread croûtons

Place the butter in a bowl and cook for 1 minute to melt. Add the onion, tossing to coat in the butter, then cover and cook for 2 minutes.

Add the mustard powder, tomatoes with their juice, chicken stock, orange juice and salt and pepper to taste. Cover and cook for 6 minutes until hot and bubbly. Liquidize in a blender until smooth or pass through a fine sieve.

Reheat by cooking for 2 minutes then serve hot, sprinkled with chopped parsley and bread croûtons.

Baked grapefruit

Serves: 4
Power setting: full
Total cooking time: 3–4 minutes

2 medium grapefruit
4 teaspoons brown sugar
2 teaspoons butter
ground cinnamon
4 maraschino cherries

Cut each grapefruit in half, remove any pips and cut around each segment with a sharp knife. Sprinkle each half with a teaspoon of sugar and dot with ½ teaspoon butter. Cook for 3–4 minutes, re-arranging half-way through the cooking time.

To serve, dust the tops of the grapefruit lightly with ground cinnamon and garnish with a cherry.

Stuffed eggs à la mornay

Serves: 4
Power setting: full
Total cooking time: 4 minutes

4 hard-boiled eggs
15g/½oz butter
50g/2oz button mushrooms, chopped
1 small onion, peeled and very finely chopped
cheese sauce (see page 121), hot
25g/1oz strong Cheddar cheese, grated
chopped parsley to garnish

Peel the hard-boiled eggs and cut in half lengthways. Remove the yolks and place in a small bowl.

Place the butter in a bowl and cook for ½ minute to melt. Add the mushrooms and onion and cook for 1½ minutes. Add to the egg yolks and mix well to blend. Stuff each egg half with an equal quantity of the mixture. Place in a flameproof serving dish. Pour over the cheese sauce and top with the grated cheese. Cook for 2 minutes or until the cheese melts. Brown under a preheated hot grill if liked, then garnish with chopped parsley.

Serve with fingers of freshly-made toast.

Speedy kipper pâté

Serves: 4
Power setting: full
Total cooking time: 5 minutes

1 170g/6 oz packet frozen cook-in-the-bag kipper fillets
40g/1½oz butter, softened
finely grated rind of ½ lemon
ground nutmeg
freshly ground black pepper

Place the kipper fillets in their bag on a plate and snip two holes in the bag to allow the steam to escape. Cook for 5 minutes.

Carefully remove the fillets from the bag and flake into a blender goblet, removing and discarding any dark skin and bones. Add the butter, lemon rind and nutmeg and pepper to taste. Purée until smooth and creamy.

Spoon into individual ramekins or dishes and cover with cling film. Chill thoroughly before serving with hot toast fingers or crisp crackers.

Baked avocado with prawns

Serves: 4
Power setting: full
Total cooking time: 3½–4½ minutes

150ml/¼ pint milk
7g/¼ oz butter
1 tablespoon flour
100g/4 oz peeled prawns
pinch of cayenne pepper
salt and freshly ground black pepper
2 teaspoons lemon juice
2 teaspoons tomato purée
2 large ripe avocado pears
1–2 tablespoons dry breadcrumbs

Place the milk in a jug and cook for ½ minute. Mix the butter with the flour and gradually whisk into the milk. Cook for 1 minute, stirring half-way through the cooking time, until thickened. Add the prawns and cayenne, salt and pepper to taste. Stir in most of the lemon juice and tomato purée, blending well.

Cut the avocados in half lengthways, remove the stones and brush with the remaining lemon juice to stop discolouration. Pile the prawn filling equally into the centre of each avocado half and sprinkle with the breadcrumbs. Place on a plate, pointed ends inwards and cook for 2–3 minutes, turning and re-arranging half-way through the cooking time. Serve hot with brown bread fingers or toast.

Smoked haddock brandade

Serves: 6–8
Power setting: full
Total cooking time: 4–5 minutes

450g/1 lb smoked haddock
2 tablespoons water
175g/6 oz butter, softened
3 tablespoons tartare sauce
2 tablespoons lemon juice
generous pinch of cayenne pepper
freshly ground black pepper
2 tablespoons chopped parsley

Place the haddock in a shallow dish with the water. Cover with cling film, snipping two holes in the top to allow the steam to escape. Cook for 4–5 minutes. Drain then allow to cool.

Remove any skin and bones from the fish and place in a blender with the remaining ingredients. Purée until smooth. Alternatively, place the fish into a bowl, beat the butter until smooth and creamy and then mix all the ingredients together, blending well. Place in a large or several small dishes and chill thoroughly. Serve with a little salad and crisp toast.

Family farmhouse pâté

Serves: 6
Power setting: full
Total cooking time: 13–14 minutes

50g/2oz butter
2 onions, peeled and chopped
2 cloves garlic, peeled and crushed
225g/8oz turkey livers, trimmed and chopped
225g/8 oz belly of pork, trimmed and chopped
175g/6 oz streaky bacon, rinds removed and chopped
2 teaspoons chopped fresh sage or mixed fresh herbs
4 tablespoons brandy or Madeira
4 tablespoons double cream
salt and freshly ground black pepper
50g/2oz clarified butter
bay leaves and fresh herbs to garnish

Place the butter in a bowl and cook for 1 minute to melt. Add the onion and garlic and cook for 5 minutes, stirring half-way through the cooking time. Add the turkey livers, pork, bacon and herbs. Cover and cook for 7–8 minutes or until the meat is cooked. Place in a blender with the brandy or Madeira and cream, and purée until smooth. Season to taste and spoon into a terrine or serving dish. Pour over the clarified butter to cover, garnish with bay leaves or fresh herbs and chill until set.

Serve with hot toast or crisp crackers.

Bacon-wrapped water chestnuts

Makes: 16
Power setting: full
Total cooking time: 6 minutes

1 240g/8½oz can water chestnuts, drained
8 rashers bacon, rinded and cut in half
4 tablespoons soy sauce
½ teaspoon ground ginger
½ teaspoon garlic powder

Wrap each water chestnut in a piece of bacon and secure with a wooden cocktail stick.

Mix the soy sauce with the ginger and garlic in a shallow dish. Add the bacon-wrapped water chestnuts and leave to marinate in the refrigerator for 4–6 hours, turning from time to time.

Drain the bacon-wrapped water chestnuts and place on a roasting rack. Cover with a sheet of absorbent kitchen towel. Cook for 3 minutes, turn and cook for a further 3 minutes.

Serve hot with drinks as an appetizer.

Devils on horseback

Makes: 30
Power setting: full
Total cooking time: 4 minutes

30 dessert prunes, pre-soaked and stoned
30 salted almonds
2 tablespoons fruit chutney
10 long thin rashers bacon, rinded

Stuff each prune with a salted almond and a little fruit chutney.

Stretch the bacon rashers with the back of a knife and cut each into three equal pieces. Place a stuffed prune on the end of each bacon strip and roll up neatly. Secure with a wooden cocktail stick.

Place on a roasting rack and cover with a sheet of absorbent kitchen towel. Cook for 4 minutes, giving the rack a half-turn half-way through the cooking time.

Serve hot as a savoury with drinks.

Hot herb and cheese dip

Serves: 4
Power setting: full
Total cooking time: 4½–5 minutes

50g/2oz butter
3 tablespoons flour
300ml/½ pint milk
100g/4 oz Cheddar cheese, grated
3 tablespoons tarragon and thyme mustard
salt and freshly ground black pepper

Place the butter in a jug and cook for 1 minute to melt. Add the flour, mixing well. Gradually add the milk, blending well. Cook for 3½–4 minutes, stirring every minute until the sauce is smooth and thickened.

Add the cheese, mustard and salt and pepper to taste, mixing well to melt the cheese.

Serve hot or cold with vegetable sticks, cooked sausages or toast fingers.

Hot horseradish tomato dip

Serves: 4
Power setting: full
Total cooking time: 3–4 minutes

1 225g/8oz can baked beans in tomato sauce
3 tablespoons horseradish mustard
1 tablespoon tomato ketchup
2 tablespoons vinegar
2 small onions, peeled and chopped

Place the ingredients in a blender goblet or food processor and blend until smooth. Place in a serving bowl and cover with cling film, snipping two holes in the top to allow the steam to escape. Cook for 3–4 minutes until hot and bubbly.

Serve hot with cooked sausages, crisp vegetables or crackers.

Fish and shellfish

Guide to cooking fish

Fish	Quantity		Cooking time in minutes on full power	Preparation
Bass	whole	450g/1lb	5–7	Shield the head and tail with foil. Cut the skin in two or three places to prevent it from bursting.
Cod	fillets	450g/1lb	5–7	Place the fillet tails to the centre of the dish or shield with foil. Cut the skin in two or three places to prevent it from bursting.
	steaks	450g/1lb	4–5	Cover with greaseproof paper before cooking.
Haddock	fillets	450g/1 lb	5–7	Cover with greaseproof paper before cooking.
Halibut	steaks	450g/1lb	4–5	Cover with greaseproof paper before cooking.
Kippers	whole	1	1–2	Cover with cling film and snip two holes in the top to allow the steam to escape.
Red mullet and Red snapper	whole	450g/1lb	5–7	Shield the head and tail with foil. Cut the skin in two or three places to prevent it from bursting.
Salmon	steaks	450g/1lb	4–5	Cover with greaseproof paper before cooking.
Salmon trout	whole	450g/1lb	7–8	Shield the head and tail with foil. Cut the skin in two or three places to prevent it from bursting.

Scallops			Cover with dampened absorbent kitchen paper.
Smoked haddock	whole	450g/1lb	4–5	Cover with cling film, snipping two holes in the top to allow the steam to escape.
Trout	whole	450g/1lb	8–9	Shield the head and tail with foil, cut the skin in two or three places to prevent it from bursting.

Guide to reheating boiled shellfish

Lobster	tails	450g/1lb	5–6	Turn tails over half-way through the cooking time. Allow to stand for 5 minutes before serving. Turn over half-way through the cooking time.
	whole	450g/1lb	6–8	
Prawns and Scampi		450g/1lb	5–6	Arrange the peeled shellfish in a ring in a shallow dish and cover with cling film, snipping two holes in the top to allow the steam to escape.
Shrimps		450g/1lb	5–6	Arrange the peeled shrimps in a ring in a shallow dish and cover with cling film, snipping two holes in the top to allow the steam to escape.

Guide to defrosting fish and shellfish

Fish	Quantity	Heating time in minutes on defrost power
Fish fillets	450g/1lb	7–8
Fish steaks	1 175g/6oz steak	2
	2 175g/6oz steaks	3–4
Whole fish	1 225–275g/8–10oz whole fish	4–6
	2 225–275g/8–10oz whole fish	10–12
	1 1.5–1.75kg/3–4 lb whole fish	20–22

Shellfish	Quantity	Heating time in minutes on defrost power
Crabmeat	450g/1lb	14–16
Lobster	450g/1lb	12
whole	675g/1½ lb	16–18 .
Prawns and Scampi	450g/1lb	7–8
Scallops	450g/1lb	8–10
Shrimps	450g/1lb	7–8

Note To defrost fish and shellfish on full power, cook for ¼–½ minute, allow to stand for 2 minutes, then repeat until evenly thawed throughout, turning and rotating the food and dish occasionally.

Soused herrings

Serves: 4
Power setting: full
Total cooking time: 6 minutes

4 herrings, each weighing about 225g/8 oz
salt
1 blade mace (optional)
1 bay leaf
6 black peppercorns
2 whole cloves
150ml/¼ pint vinegar or lemon juice
150ml/¼ pint water
1 onion, peeled and sliced into rings

Clean, gut and bone the herrings. Trim the heads, tails and fins from
the fish and season with a little salt. Roll up, skin-side out, from the
tail ends and secure with wooden cocktail sticks. Place in a single
layer in a shallow dish with the mace, bay leaf, peppercorns and
cloves. Pour over the vinegar or lemon juice and top with the onion.

Cover with cling film, snipping two holes in the top to allow the
steam to escape, and cook for 6 minutes, giving the dish a half-turn
after 3 minutes. Leave the herrings to cool in the liquor then chill
lightly in the refrigerator. Drain before serving.

Cold smoked haddock soufflé

Serves: 4
Power setting: full
Total cooking time: 14 minutes

225g/8 oz boil-in-the-bag frozen haddock, fillet
1 small onion, peeled and chopped
grated rind of 1 lemon
1 tablespoon lemon juice
50g/2 oz butter
50g/2 oz plain flour
600ml/1 pint milk
1 tablespoon chopped fresh parsley
4 eggs, separated
freshly ground black pepper

15g/½oz powdered gelatine
2 tablespoons hot water
To garnish:
chopped parsley
lemon slices

Remove the haddock from the bag and place in a dish with the onion, lemon rind and lemon juice. Cook for 3 minutes, turn the fish over and cook for a further 3 minutes.

Place the butter in a bowl and cook for 1 minute to melt. Stir in the flour and cook for ½ minute.

Place the milk in a jug and cook for 3 minutes until very hot. Gradually add to the roux mixture, blending well. Cook for 3 minutes, stirring every minute to keep the sauce smooth. Allow to cool slightly.

Remove any skin and bones from the fish and place in a blender with the onion and any cooking juices. Purée until smooth and blend in the parsley, egg yolks and sauce. Season with pepper to taste. Place the gelatine in a bowl with the water and cook for ½ minute until clear and dissolved. Add to the fish mixture and chill until almost set.

Meanwhile, prepare a small 14cm/5in soufflé dish by tying a double band of greaseproof paper around the upper edge of the dish, leaving about 5cm/2in above the rim.

Whisk the egg whites until they stand in stiff peaks and fold into the fish mixture with a metal spoon. Pour into the soufflé dish and chill until set.

To serve, carefully remove the greaseproof paper with a hot knife. Press the chopped parsley around the top edge of the soufflé and garnish the top with slices of lemon. Serve with crisp toast.

Poached salmon steaks Hollandaise

Serves: 4
Power setting: full
Total cooking time: 6–8 minutes

4 salmon steaks, cut 2.5cm/1in thick
8 tablespoons water
1 tablespoon lemon juice
salt and freshly ground white pepper

To serve:
Hollandaise sauce (see page 124)

Wipe the salmon steaks, tucks in the flaps of skin and secure to a neat shape with wooden cocktail sticks. Place in a shallow dish and add the water and lemon juice. Season with salt and pepper to taste. Cover with cling film, snipping two holes in the top to allow any steam to escape, and cook for 6–8 minutes, turning the dish twice during the cooking time. Allow to stand for 5 minutes before serving with the Hollandaise sauce.

Kedgeree

Serves: 4
Power setting: full
Total cooking time: 11–15 minutes

350g/12oz smoked haddock fillet
75g/3 oz butter
2 tablespoons water
3 hard-boiled eggs, shelled
450g/1lb cooked long-grain rice
salt
cayenne pepper
To garnish:
chopped parsley

Place the smoked haddock in a dish with 15g/½oz of the butter and the water. Cover and cook for 6–8 minutes until tender, giving the dish a half turn after 3 minutes. Remove any skin and bones from the fish and flake coarsely.

Chop two of the eggs and slice the third into rings. Place the remaining butter in a dish and cook for 1 minute to melt. Stir in the fish, chopped eggs, cooked rice and salt and cayenne pepper to taste. Cook for 4–6 minutes, stirring twice, until very hot.

Stir in a little chopped parsley and pile on to a warmed serving plate. Garnish with lines of chopped parsley and the sliced hard-boiled egg. Serve at once.

Poached and glazed salmon trout

Serves: 8–10
Power setting: full
Total cooking time: 28½ minutes

1 1.75kg/4lb salmon trout, gutted
2 tablespoons lemon juice
4 tablespoons boiling water
600ml/1pint liquid aspic jelly
a little cucumber skin, cut into thin strips
a few small radishes, trimmed and thinly sliced
1 teaspoon powdered gelatine
2 tablespoons cold water
450ml/¾pint mayonnaise
To garnish:
watercress sprigs
cucumber slices
lemon slices

Place the salmon in a shallow dish with the lemon juice and boiling water. Prick the salmon skin in several places to prevent it from bursting during cooking. Cover with cling film, snipping two holes in the top to allow the steam to escape. Cook for 28 minutes, giving the dish a quarter-turn every 7 minutes.

Remove the cling film and allow to cool. Remove and discard the skin from the salmon then place on a serving plate. Brush the fish with the liquid aspic. Arrange pieces of cucumber skin and radish slices along the length of the fish, dipping into aspic before placing on the fish. Allow to set.

Remove any aspic jelly that has collected around the base of the fish and discard. Spoon the remaining jelly over the fish and 'flood' the serving dish with a thin layer. Leave to set.

Sprinkle the gelatine in the cold water in a small bowl and leave to soften for 5 minutes. Cook for ½ minute until clear and dissolved. Stir into the mayonnaise and chill for about 15 minutes until thickened.

Place the thickened mayonnaise in a piping bag fitted with a large star-shaped nozzle and pipe swirls along the length of the fish. Garnish with watercress sprigs, cucumber and lemon slices if liked.

Crab in sherry and brandy

Serves: 4
Power setting: full
Total cooking time: 12½ minutes

25g/1oz butter
1½ tablespoons oil
1 clove garlic, peeled and crushed
1 large onion, peeled and finely chopped
1 large tomato, peeled, seeded and chopped
1 tablespoon dry sherry
1 tablespoon brandy
225g/8oz crabmeat
1½ tablespoons chicken stock
1 tablespoon finely chopped parsley
pinch of cayenne pepper
salt
Breadcrumbs:
25g/1oz butter
2 tablespoons fresh soft white breadcrumbs
To garnish:
lemon wedges
parsley sprigs

Place the butter and oil in a medium-sized dish and cook for ½ minute. Add the garlic and onion and cook for 3 minutes. Stir in the tomato, sherry and brandy and cook, uncovered, for 3 minutes, stirring half-way through the cooking time.

Stir in the crab, chicken stock, parsley and cayenne and salt to taste. Cook for 1 minute.

To make the browned breadcrumbs place the butter in a bowl and cook for ½ minute to melt. Add the breadcrumbs and toss in the butter. Cook for ½ minute. Stir well then cook for a further 2 minutes or until the crumbs are golden. Sprinkle on top of the crab mixture and cook for a further 2 minutes.

Serve immediately in individual scallop shells garnished with lemon wedges and sprigs of parsley.

Coquilles St Jacques

Serves: 4
Power setting: full
Total cooking time: 8 minutes

50g/2oz butter
2 tablespoons finely chopped spring onions
40g/1½oz plain flour
100g/4oz button mushrooms, sliced
5 tablespoons dry white wine
5 tablespoons milk
salt and freshly ground white pepper
450g/1lb prepared scallops
25g/1oz Cheddar cheese, grated
To garnish:
chopped parsley
lemon butterflies

Place the butter and spring onions in a large dish and cook for 3 minutes. Add the flour and stir well to blend. Cook for ½ minute, stir again and cook for a further ½ minute.

Add the mushrooms, wine, milk, salt and pepper to taste, scallops and cheese, mixing well. Cover and cook for 4 minutes stirring every minute. At the end of the cooking time the scallops will be coated with a thick creamy sauce.

Serve hot in individual scallop shells or mornay dishes, sprinkled with chopped parsley and garnished with lemon butterflies.

Prawns creole

Serves: 4
Power setting: full
Total cooking time: 12–13 minutes

1 small onion, peeled and finely chopped
1 small green pepper, cored, seeded and chopped
25g/1oz butter
2–3 tablespoons flour
1 425g/15oz can peeled tomatoes
1 225g/8 oz can peeled tomatoes
1 teaspoon dried rosemary

1 teaspoon dried oregano
1 teaspoon dried thyme
salt and freshly ground black pepper
2 teaspoons sugar
450g/1lb peeled prawns

Place the onion, pepper and butter in a bowl and cook for 4 minutes until soft. Stir in the flour, blending well, then gradually add the tomatoes, herbs, salt and pepper to taste, and sugar. Cook for 6 minutes, stirring half-way through the cooking time.

Add the prawns, blending well, and cook for a further 2–3 minutes. Serve hot with boiled rice.

Mussels in cider

Serves: 2
Power setting: full
Total cooking time: 11 minutes

1 tablespoon oil
1 small onion, peeled and chopped
1 clove garlic, peeled and crushed
1 tablespoon chopped fresh parsley
1 tablespoon plain flour
300ml/½ pint dry cider
salt and freshly ground black pepper
2.25l/2 quarts mussels, scrubbed and sorted

Place the oil, onion, garlic and parsley in a large bowl and cook for 1 minute. Blend in the flour and then the cider, mixing well. Season with salt and pepper to taste then cook for 2 minutes, stirring every ½ minute to keep the sauce smooth.

Add half of the prepared mussels, tossing well to coat in the sauce. Cover with cling film, snipping two holes in the top to allow the steam to escape, and cook for 4 minutes, stirring half-way through the cooking time. Remove with a slotted spoon and place in a heated serving dish. Discard any mussels that do not open.

Add the remaining mussels to the remaining sauce and toss to coat. Cover and cook for 4 minutes, stirring half-way through the cooking time. Add to the mussels previously cooked and serve at once.

Meat, game and poultry

Guide to cooking meat

Type and cut of meat		Cooking time in minutes on medium power per 450g/1lb or for quantity given	Cooking time in minutes on full power per 450g/1lb or for quantity given	Preparation
Beef				
–topside	rare	12	5–6	Use good quality meat with an even covering of fat and a neat shape. Allow to stand for 15–20 minutes, wrapped in foil, before carving.
	medium	14	6½–7½	
	well done	16	8½–9½	
–sirloin	rare	12	5–6	
	medium	14	6½–7½	
	well done	16	8½–9½	
–rib	rare	12–13	5½–6½	Ideally, bone and roll the joint before cooking. Allow to stand for 15–30 minutes, wrapped in foil, before carving.
	medium	14–15	7–8	
	well done	16–17	8–10	
–minced beef		14–16	10–12	
–rump steak	rare		2	Preheat a browning dish according to the manufacturer's instructions. Add the meat and brown. Turn over and cook for the recommended time.
	medium		3–4	
	well done		4	
–fillet steak	rare		2	
	medium		2–3	
	well done		3	

–braising steak		16–17	10	Ideally, cook on medium power. If using full power, leave to rest for 10 minutes half-way through the cooking time.
–hamburgers	1 100g/4oz		2–3	Preheat a browning dish according to the manufacturer's instructions. Add the hamburgers and cook for the recommended time, turning the small burgers over half-way through the cooking time, and turning the large burgers over twice during the cooking time.
	2 100g/4oz		3–4	
	3 100g/4oz		4–5	
	4 100g/4oz		5–6	
	1 225g/8oz		2½–3½	
	2 225g/8oz		6–7	
Lamb				
–leg	on bone	11–13	8–10	Choose a good quality joint. Roll the meat into a neat shape if it is off the bone. Cover the pointed end with foil to protect it if on the bone. Allow to stand for 25–30 minutes, wrapped in foil, before carving.
	off bone	12–13	9–10	
–breast		14–16	12	Roll and stuff, if liked, before cooking. Allow to stand for 30 minutes, wrapped in foil, before carving.
–crown roast			5	Cover tips of bone with foil during cooking.
–loin of lamb		11–13	8–10	Choose a good quality joint. Roll into a neat shape if boned. Allow to stand for 25–30 minutes, wrapped in foil, before carving.
–chops	loin or 2		6–7	Preheat the browning dish according to the manufacturer's instructions. Add the chops and cook for the recommended time, turning over half-way through the cooking time.
	chump 4		7–9	
	6		15–17	

Cut				Notes
Pork				
–leg		13–15	10	Choose a good quality joint. Cover the pointed end with foil to protect from over-cooking. Score fat with a sharp knife and sprinkle liberally with salt to get a crisp crackling. Allow to stand for 20 minutes, wrapped in foil, before carving. Brown under a hot grill if liked.
–loin		14–16	10–13	Roll into a neat shape before cooking. Allow to stand for 20 minutes, wrapped in foil, before carving.
–fillet			7	
–chops	loin or chump			Preheat the browning dish according to the manufacturer's instructions. Add the chops and cook for the recommended time, turning over half-way through the cooking time.
	2	14–18		
	3	19–24		
	4	26–32		
	6	33–37		
Veal				
–leg or shoulder joint		11–12	8½–9	Secure into a neat shape before cooking. Allow to stand for 20 minutes, wrapped in foil, before carving.
Bacon or gammon				
–joint		11–12		
–gammon steaks (each)		14		Cook in a browning dish if liked (observing preheating times) or cover with cling film. Turn half-way through the cooking time.

				Preparation
–bacon	4 slices 450g/1lb		3½–4 12–14	Place on a plate or bacon rack and cover with absorbent kitchen paper. Turn rashers over half-way through cooking.
Liver			5–6	
Kidney			7–8	
Sausages	2		1½–2	Prick thoroughly and arrange on a rack or plate. Cover with absorbent kitchen paper and turn half-way through the cooking time.
	4		3–3½	

Guide to roasting poultry and game

Poultry/Game	Cooking time in minutes on full power per 450g/1lb	Cooking time in minutes on medium power per 450g/1lb	Preparation
Chicken –whole	6–8	9–10	Shield the tips of the wings and legs with foil. Place in a roasting bag in a dish with 2–3 tablespoons stock. Give the dish a half-turn half-way through the cooking time.
–pieces 1	2–4		Place the meatiest part of the chicken piece to the outside of the dish. Cover with greaseproof paper. Give the dish a half-turn half-way through the cooking time.
2	4–6		
3	5–7		
4	6½–10		
5	7½–12		
6	8–14		

Duck –whole	7–8	9–11	Shield the tips of the wings, tail end and legs with foil. Prick the skin thoroughly to help release the fat. Place in a dish in a roasting bag on a trivel or upturned saucer and turn over half-way through the cooking time.
Grouse, guinea fowl, partridge, pheasant, pigeon, poussin, quail and woodcock	6–8	9–11	Shield the tips of the wings and legs with foil. Smear the breast with a little butter and place in a roasting bag in a dish. Turn the dish half-way through the cooking time.
Turkey	9–11	11–13	Shield the tips of the wings and legs with foil. Place in a roasting bag in a dish with 2–3 tablespoons stock. Turn over at least once during the cooking time and give the dish a quarter turn every 15 minutes.

Guide to defrosting meat

Meat	Defrosting time in minutes on defrost power per 450g/1lb	Preparation
Beef –joints	9	Turn over at least once during the defrosting time.

		Preparation
steaks (large)	8	
steaks (small)	4	
minced beef	10	Break up with a fork during the defrosting time.
Lamb		
—joints	10	Turn over at least once during the defrosting time.
—chops	5	
Pork		
—joints	8½	Turn over at least once during the defrosting time.
—chops	5	
Veal		
—joints	9	Turn over at least once during the defrosting time.
Kidney	4	Turn over at least once during the defrosting time.
Liver	4	Turn over at least once during the defrosting time.

Note: If your microwave does not have defrost power, then cook meat on full power for 1 minute for every 450g/1lb and leave to stand for 10 minutes to defrost. Repeat until the meat is thoroughly thawed.

Guide to defrosting poultry and game

Poultry/Game	Cooking time in minutes on defrost power per 450g/1lb	Preparation

Chicken		
–whole	6	Shield the wing tips with foil. Give the dish a quarter-turn every 1½ minutes. Remove the giblets at the end of the defrosting time.
–pieces	5	Place the meatiest part of the chicken pieces to the outside of the dish. Turn over half-way through the defrosting time.
Duck	4–6	Shield the wings, tail end and legs with foil. Give the dish a quarter-turn every 1½ minutes. Remove the giblets at the end of the defrosting time.
Grouse, guinea fowl, partridge, pheasant, pigeon, poussin, quail and woodcock	5–6	Shield the tips of the wings and legs with foil. Turn over half-way through the defrosting time and give the dish a quarter-turn every 1½ minutes.
Turkey	10–12	Shield the tips of the wings and legs with foil. Turn over twice during the defrosting time and give the dish a quarter-turn every 6 minutes. Shield any warm spots with foil during defrosting. Remove the giblets at the end of the defrosting time.

Note To defrost poultry and game on full power, cook for 1 minute per 450g/1lb, allow to stand for 10 minutes, then continue cooking in bursts of 1 minute per 450g/1lb until the poultry or game is thawed.

Boeuf Bourguignonne

Serves: 4
Power setting: full and medium
Total cooking time: 64½ minutes

25g/1oz butter
4 rashers bacon, rinded and cut into strips
1 onion, peeled and finely chopped
450g/1lb chuck steak, cubed
300ml/½ pint beef stock
150ml/¼ pint dry red wine
1 clove garlic, peeled and crushed
1 bouquet garni
salt and freshly ground black pepper
8 button onions, peeled
100g/4 oz button mushrooms
To garnish:
chopped parsley

Place the butter in a bowl and cook on full power for ½ minute. Add the bacon and chopped onion and cook on full power for 4 minutes. Remove from the oven and preheat a browning dish on full power for 5 minutes, or according to the manufacturer's instructions. Add the steak and onion mixture and turn quickly on all sides to brown evenly. Cook on full power for 5 minutes.

Transfer to a large casserole and stir in the stock, red wine, garlic, bouquet garni and salt and pepper to taste. Cover and cook on medium power for 35 minutes. Add the button onions and mushrooms and continue to cook on medium power for a further 15 minutes. Leave to stand for 5 minutes before serving garnished with chopped parsley.

Beef Stroganoff

Serves: 4
Power setting: full
Total cooking time: 14½ minutes

25g/1oz butter
675g/1½lb beef fillet, cut into thin strips
1 large onion, peeled and finely chopped

225g/8 oz button mushrooms, sliced
25g/1oz flour
100ml/4fl oz dry white wine
salt and freshly ground black pepper
150ml/¼ pint soured cream
chopped parsley to garnish

Preheat a large browning dish for 5 minutes, or according to the manufacturer's instructions. Add the butter and beef and stir quickly to brown evenly. Cook for 3 minutes, stirring half-way through the cooking time.

Remove the meat from the dish with a slotted spoon. Add the onions and mushrooms to the juices and cook for 4½ minutes, stirring after 2 minutes. Stir in the flour, blending well, then gradually add the wine. Add the meat and salt and pepper to taste then cook for 2 minutes. Stir in the soured cream, blending well. Serve at once, garnished with chopped parsley. Ideal accompaniments are boiled rice or pasta and a crisp salad.

Teriyaki beef and bacon burgers

Serves: 4
Power setting: full
Total cooking time: 12–13 minutes

8 rashers streaky bacon, rinded
450g/1lb lean minced beef
salt and freshly ground black pepper
4 tablespoons soy sauce
2 tablespoons lemon juice
2 tablespoons clear honey
2 tablespoons dry white wine
1 clove garlic, peeled and crushed
pinch of ground ginger

Place the bacon on a bacon rack or plate and cook for 2 minutes.

Season the beef with salt and pepper to taste then form into four burgers. Wrap two rashers of bacon around each burger and secure with wooden cocktail sticks. Place in a shallow dish. Combine the remaining ingredients and pour over the burgers. Cover and leave to marinate in the refrigerator for 4–6 hours.

To cook, preheat a large browning dish for 5 minutes or according to the manufacturer's instructions. Add the burgers and brown quickly on both sides. Cook for 5–6 minutes, turning over half-way through the cooking time.

Serve at once with a crisp green salad.

Savoury meatballs in tomato sauce

Serves: 4
Power setting: full
Total cooking time: 18 minutes

450g/1lb lean minced beef
25g/1oz fresh white breadcrumbs
1 onion, peeled and grated
1 teaspoon dried mixed herbs
salt and freshly ground black pepper
beaten egg
Sauce:
75g/3oz butter
1 onion, peeled and chopped
50g/2oz mushrooms, sliced
40g/1½oz flour
150ml/¼ pint hot water
1 beef stock cube
1 398g/14oz can peeled tomatoes, roughly chopped

Mix the beef, breadcrumbs, onion, herbs and salt and pepper to taste, with enough egg to bind the mixture. Divide into eight portions and form into meatballs. Arrange in a shallow dish and cook for 8 minutes, turning the meatballs once and giving the dish a half-turn half-way through the cooking time.

To make the sauce, dice half of the butter and place in a bowl. Add the onion and mushrooms and cook for 2 minutes. Add the remaining butter and cook for 1 minute. Add the flour, blending well. Gradually add the hot water and stir in the crumbled stock cube. Add the tomatoes and cook for 4 minutes, stirring half-way through the cooking time. Season to taste, and pour over the meatballs. Cook for a further 3 minutes.

Serve hot with fluffy rice and a salad.

Spicy meatloaf

Serves: 4
Power setting: full
Total cooking time: 16 minutes

1 tablespoon oil
1 onion, peeled and finely chopped
350g/12oz minced beef
100g/4oz sausagemeat
2 teaspoons chopped fresh herbs or 1 teaspoon dried
1 tablespoon tomato ketchup
25g/1oz fresh white breadcrumbs
salt and freshly ground black pepper
1 egg, beaten

Place the oil in a bowl and cook for 1 minute. Add the onion, mixing well, and cook for 3 minutes, stirring after 2 minutes. Add the beef, sausagemeat, herbs, ketchup, breadcrumbs and salt and pepper to taste, blending well. Bind together with the beaten egg then press firmly into a loaf dish. Cook for 7 minutes, giving the dish a half-turn half-way through the cooking time. Cover with foil and leave to stand for 5 minutes.

Uncover and cook for a further 5 minutes. Re-wrap in foil and leave to stand for 3 minutes.

Serve hot, in slices, with a tomato sauce and jacket potatoes or with a salad.

Cowboy hash

Serves: 6
Power setting: full
Total cooking time: 28–31 minutes

2 tablespoons oil
1 medium onion, peeled and chopped
675g/1½lb lean minced beef
2 tablespoons tomato purée
150ml/¼ pint beef stock
salt and freshly ground black pepper
2 450g/1lb cans baked beans with sausages

6 slices toasted bread
chopped parsley to garnish

Place the oil in a large bowl and cook for 1 minute. Add the onion, mixing well, and cook for a further 2 minutes. Add the beef and cook for a further 15 minutes, stirring and breaking up every 5 minutes.

Add the tomato purée, beef stock and salt and pepper to taste. Cover and cook for 5 minutes.

Add the beans with sausages, blending well. Cover and cook for 5–8 minutes or until hot and bubbly.

Meanwhile, remove the crusts from the bread and cut the slices into triangles. Serve the hash surrounded with the bread triangles and sprinkled with chopped parsley.

Tacos with beef and beans

Serves: 6
Power setting: full
Total cooking time: 19–20 minutes

2 tablespoons oil
1 small onion, peeled and finely chopped
350g/12oz minced beef
2 green peppers, cored, seeded and chopped
2 tablespoons taco sauce
2 tablespoons red wine
salt and freshly ground black pepper
1 450g/1lb can baked beans in tomato sauce
6 ready-made taco shells
6 black olives to garnish

Place the oil and onion in a bowl and cook for 2 minutes. Add the beef and cook for 6 minutes, stirring and breaking up the meat every 2 minutes. Add the taco sauce, red wine and salt and pepper to taste. Cover and cook for a further 5 minutes. Add the beans, blending well, and cook for 4–5 minutes until very hot and bubbly.

Fill the taco shells with the hot beef and bean mixture and garnish each with a black olive.

Barbecued bean tostadas

Serves: 6
Power setting: full
Total cooking time: 9–11 minutes

2 450g/1lb cans barbecued beans
275g/10oz chopped cooked chicken
salt and freshly ground black pepper
6 tostada shells
To garnish:
finely chopped cucumber
finely chopped red pepper
sprigs of parsley

Place the beans, chicken and salt and pepper to taste in a bowl. Cover and cook for 8–10 minutes until very hot and bubbly.

Place the tostada shells on a plate and cook for 1 minute to warm. Spoon the chicken and bean mixture on to each warmed tostada and sprinkle with the cucumber and red pepper. Garnish with a sprig of parsley and serve at once.

Oriental roast loin of pork

Serves: 4–6
Power setting: medium
Total cooking time: 42–48 minutes

1 1.5kg/3lb loin of pork, boned and rolled
2 teaspoons mustard powder
Marinade:
100ml/4fl oz dry sherry
100ml/4fl oz soy sauce
1 tablespoon grated root ginger or 2 teaspoons ground ginger
2 cloves garlic, peeled and crushed

Rub the pork with the mustard powder and place in a large dish. Mix the marinade ingredients together and pour over the pork. Leave to marinate for at least 2 hours, turning occasionally.

Place the pork on a roasting rack and cook for 42–48 minutes, turning over half-way through the cooking time and giving the dish a quarter turn every 10 minutes. Wrap in foil and allow to stand for

15–20 minutes before carving.

Serve thickly sliced with new potatoes and a coleslaw salad.

Piquant pork casserole

Serves: 4
Power setting: full and medium
Total cooking time: 1 hour 11 minutes

675g/1½lb shoulder of pork
50g/2oz plain flour
salt and freshly ground black pepper
2 tablespoons oil
2 onions, peeled and chopped
4 carrots, peeled and sliced
1 green pepper, cored, seeded and sliced
300 ml/½ pint meat stock
1 bouquet garni
small piece of lemon peel
dash of Tabasco sauce
100g/4oz button mushrooms

Cut the meat into 3.5cm/1½in cubes. Mix the flour with salt and pepper to taste and toss the meat in this mixture. Preheat a browning dish on full power for 5 minutes or according to the manufacturer's instructions. Add the oil and cook on full power for 1 minute. Add the pork, turning quickly on all sides to brown evenly and cook on full power for a further 5 minutes.

Transfer to a large casserole and add the onions, carrots, peppers, meat stock, bouquet garni, lemon peel and Tabasco sauce, blending well. Cover and cook on medium power for 45 minutes.

Add the mushrooms and continue to cook on medium power for a further 15 minutes. Leave to stand for 5 minutes before serving.

Pork fillet with green onions

Serves: 4
Power setting: full
Total cooking time: 16–17 minutes

675g/1½lb pork fillet, thinly sliced into rounds
1 tablespoon sherry
1 teaspoon cornflour
2 tablespoons soy sauce
3 tablespoons clear honey
1 tablespoon vinegar
6 spring onions, trimmed and cut into 2.5cm/1in pieces
2 tablespoons oil
100g/4oz frozen peas
4 tomatoes, quartered

Place the pork in a bowl with the sherry, cornflour, soy sauce, honey, vinegar and onions, blending well. Cover and leave to marinate for 20–30 minutes.

Meanwhile, preheat a large browning dish for 5 minutes, or according to the manufacturer's instructions. Add the oil and cook for a further 1 minute. Add the pork mixture and juices and cook for 7 minutes, stirring every 2 minutes.

Stir in the peas and tomatoes and cook for a further 3–4 minutes until cooked but still firm. Serve at once.

Devilled lamb parcels

Serves: 4
Power setting: full
Total cooking time: 8–10 minutes

25g/1oz butter
2 tablespoons French mustard
2 tablespoons chopped parsley
1 clove garlic, peeled and crushed
1 tablespoon capers
pinch of cayenne pepper
2 teaspoons lemon juice
salt and freshly ground black pepper
4 lamb shoulder steaks
1 small onion, peeled and sliced into rings

Beat the butter with the mustard, parsley, garlic, capers, cayenne, lemon juice and salt and pepper to taste.

Spread each lamb steak with an equal quantity of the butter and place in a small cook-in-the-bag with a quarter of the onion rings.

Secure loosely at the neck with an elastic band or string. Place on a plate and cook for 8–10 minutes until cooked. Allow to stand for 5 minutes before serving the steaks snipped from their 'parcels'.

Spring crown of lamb

Serves: 6–8
Power setting: full
Total cooking time: 26–30 minutes

1 crown roast of lamb with about 14–16 cutlets
Stuffing:
1 tablespoon oil
1 small onion, peeled and chopped
1 stalk celery, chopped
100g/4oz carrots, peeled and chopped
25g/1oz sultanas
450g/1lb cooking apples, peeled, cored and chopped
50g/2 oz cooked rice
2 tablespoons chopped fresh parsley
salt and freshly ground black pepper
lemon juice

Trim the lamb neatly and place on a microwave roasting rack or upturned saucer in a large shallow dish. Cover loosely with absorbent kitchen towel and cook for 10 minutes, then allow to stand while making the stuffing.

Place the oil, onion, celery, carrots, sultanas and apples in a dish. Cover and cook for 6–8 minutes until softened but still firm. Add the rice, parsley, salt, pepper and lemon juice to taste, blending well.

Place the stuffing in the centre of the crown roast and cover the tips of the bones with a little foil.

Cook for a further 10–12 minutes before carving.

To serve, place the roast on a warmed serving plate and fit cutlet frills to the tips of the bones. Carve down between the bones, allowing 2–3 ribs per person. Serve with new potatoes, mint jelly and a gravy made from the cooking juices (made with a little apple juice or cider if liked).

Minted lamb platter

Serves: 4
Power setting: full
Total cooking time: 5 minutes

1 best end of lamb, about 8 cutlets, chined
salt and freshly ground black pepper
150ml/¼ pint aspic jelly
1 teaspoon fresh garden mint sauce
Salad:
350g/12oz grated carrot
1 large green dessert apple, cored and chopped
1 tablespoon raisins
25g/1oz hazelnuts, chopped
2 teaspoons fresh garden mint sauce
2 teaspoons lemon juice
1 tablespoon castor sugar

Place the meat on a roasting rack and cover the tips of the bones with a little foil. Season with salt and pepper to taste then cook for 5 minutes, giving the dish a half-turn after 3 minutes. Cover with foil and leave until completely cold. Carefully cut the meat into 8 cutlets. Mix the aspic jelly with the mint sauce and cool until a thin coating consistency is obtained. Spoon over the cutlets and leave in a cool place to set.

Meanwhile, mix the carrot with the apple, raisins and hazelnuts. Beat the mint sauce with the lemon juice and sugar. Pour over the salad mixture and toss well. Season to taste with salt and pepper.

To serve, arrange the cutlets attractively on a plate and garnish with the salad.

Kidneys in raisin sauce

Serves: 2
Power setting: full
Total cooking time: 13 minutes

50g/2 oz butter
6 lamb's kidneys, skinned, cored and thinly sliced
1 onion, peeled and finely chopped
100g/4oz button mushrooms, sliced

25g/1oz flour
300ml/½ pint stock
50g/2 oz raisins
salt and freshly ground black pepper
½ teaspoon dried mixed herbs

Place the butter in a bowl and cook for 1 minute to melt. Stir in the kidneys and cook, uncovered, for 2 minutes. Remove the kidneys with a slotted spoon and reserve.

Add the onion and mushrooms to the juices and cook for 2 minutes. Stir in the flour then gradually add the stock, blending well. Add the raisins, salt and pepper to taste and the herbs. Cook for 3 minutes, stirring every minute to keep the sauce smooth.

Add the kidneys, cover and cook for 5 minutes, stirring half-way through the cooking time. Serve with boiled rice.

Kidneys in red wine

Serves: 3–4
Power setting: full
Total cooking time: 10½–12½ minutes

25g/1oz butter
8 lamb's kidneys, skinned, cored and quartered
1 onion, peeled and chopped
225g/8oz button mushrooms, sliced
50g/2oz flour
1 teaspoon dried oregano
4 ripe tomatoes, peeled, seeded and chopped
150ml/¼ pint dry red wine
salt and freshly ground black pepper
chopped parsley to garnish

Place the butter in a bowl and cook for ½ minute to melt. Stir in the kidneys, onion and mushrooms, cover and cook for 6–8 minutes, stirring half-way through the cooking time.

Stir in the flour, oregano, tomatoes, wine and salt and pepper to taste, blending well. Cover and cook for 4 minutes, stirring every minute. Serve hot on a bed of cooked rice. Garnish with chopped parsley.

Devilled Danish steaks

Serves: 4
Power setting: full and defrost
Total cooking time: 12–14 minutes

4 175g/6oz Danish gammon steaks
25g/1oz butter
1 onion, peeled and finely chopped
1 tablespoon tomato purée
1 teaspoon mustard powder
1 teaspoon ground paprika
1 tablespoon soft brown sugar
2 tablespoons Worcestershire sauce
2 tablespoons wine vinegar
To garnish:
4 slices fresh pineapple
watercress sprigs

Snip the rind of the gammon steaks at 2.5cm/1in intervals. Place in large shallow dish and dot with the butter. Cook on full power for 4 minutes. Remove the gammon steaks from the dish with a slotted spoon and set aside.

Stir the onion into the pan juices and cook on full power for 2 minutes. Add the tomato purée, mustard powder, paprika, brown sugar, Worcestershire sauce and wine vinegar, blending well. Return the gammon steaks to the dish. Cook, uncovered, on defrost power, for 6–8 minutes.

Serve hot, garnished with the pineapple slices and watercress sprigs. Creamed potatoes or cooked rice make an ideal accompaniment.

Chicken and Camembert

Serves: 4
Power setting: medium
Total cooking time: 27–30 minutes

1 1.5kg/3lb roasting chicken
2 small Camembert cheese portions, sliced
25g/1oz butter
salt and freshly ground black pepper

Carefully loosen the skin from the breast of the chicken and stuff with the Camembert cheese slices. Secure back in place with wooden cocktail sticks. Dot with the butter and season generously with salt and pepper.

Place in a roasting bag on a roasting rack or upturned saucer and cook for 27–30 minutes, giving the dish a half-turn half-way through the cooking time. Allow to stand for 5 minutes before carving.

Chicken cordon bleu

Serves: 4
Power setting: full
Total cooking time: 13–15 minutes

2 225g/8 oz boned chicken breasts
100g/4 oz thinly-sliced Swiss cheese
100g/4oz thinly-sliced ham
50g/2oz flour
1 egg, lightly beaten
fresh white breadcrumbs to coat
2 tablespoons oil

Cut each chicken breast in half and flatten by pounding with a mallet or rolling pin on a chopping board.

Stack alternate layers of ham and cheese together until the pile is about 1.5cm/½in thick. Press firmly together, then cut into four sticks, each 7.5cm/3in long by about 1.5cm/½in wide. Place one ham and cheese stick in the centre of each chicken slice. Roll the chicken lengthwise over the ham and cheese and secure with a wooden cocktail stick. Roll in the flour and dip in the beaten egg to coat. Toss in the breadcrumbs to coat evenly. Chill thoroughly.

Preheat a browning dish for 5 minutes or according to the manufacturer's instructions. Add the oil and cook for a further 1 minute. Add the chicken and brown on all sides. Drain on absorbent kitchen towel. Place in a shallow dish and cook for 6–8 minutes or until the chicken is tender. Leave to stand for 2 minutes. Remove and discard the cocktail sticks before serving.

Tandoori chicken wings

Serves: 4
Power setting: medium
Total cooking time: 20–22 minutes

12 chicken wings
6 tablespoons vinegar
300ml/½ pint natural yoghurt
4 cloves garlic, peeled
2 onions, peeled and quartered
100g/4oz root ginger, peeled
juice of 1 lemon
2 teaspoons garam masala
1 teaspoon chilli powder
few drops of yellow colouring
1½ teaspoons salt
To garnish:
shredded lettuce
tomato slices
onion rings

Wipe the chicken wings and make two deep cuts into the flesh of each.
Place in a shallow baking dish.

Place the vinegar, yoghurt, garlic, onions, root ginger, lemon juice,
garam masala, chilli powder, paprika, colouring and salt in a blender
goblet. Purée until smooth then pour over the chicken wings. Cover
and chill for 24 hours, turning the wings occasionally in the tandoori
marinade.

Cook, uncovered, for 20–22 minutes, turning and re-arranging the
chicken wings every 5 minutes.

Serve hot or cold garnished with shredded lettuce, tomato slices
and onion rings.

Chicken breasts in rum and orange sauce

Serves: 4
Power setting: full
Total cooking time: 13–15 minutes

4 boneless chicken breasts
1 tablespoon seasoned flour

1 tablespoon oil
40g/1½oz butter
grated rind of 2 oranges
juice of 3 oranges
4 tablespoons brown rum
4 tablespoons double cream
orange slices or segments to garnish

Toss the chicken breasts in the seasoned flour to coat lightly.

Preheat a large browning dish for 5 minutes, or according to the manufacturer's instructions. Add the oil and butter and swirl to melt. Add the chicken breasts, moving them round quickly and turning them over so that they brown evenly. Cook for 6½–8 minutes or until cooked.

Remove the chicken breasts from the dish with a slotted spoon and place on a heated serving dish. Add the orange rind, orange juice, rum and cream to the juices, blending well. Cook for 1½–2 minutes until hot and bubbly.

Spoon over the chicken breasts and serve garnished with orange slices or segments.

Turkey vindaloo

Serves: 4
Power setting: full
Total cooking time: 30 minutes

3 tablespoons oil
2 large onions, peeled and sliced
1–2 green chillies, seeded and sliced
25g/1oz root ginger, peeled and finely chopped
3 cloves garlic, peeled and crushed
1½ teaspoons ground turmeric
1 teaspoon ground coriander
1 teaspoon garam masala
2 tablespoons vinegar
200ml/7fl oz chicken stock
900g/2lb turkey thigh meat, skinned and cut into bite-sized pieces
½ teaspoon salt
50g/2oz desiccated coconut

Place the oil, onions, chillies, root ginger, garlic, turmeric, coriander and garam masala in a large bowl and cook, uncovered, for 6 minutes, stirring half-way through the cooking time.

Add the vinegar, chicken stock, turkey meat and salt, blending well. Cover and cook for 20 minutes, stirring every 5 minutes.

Add the coconut, blending well, and cook, uncovered, for a further 4 minutes. Allow to stand for 5 minutes before serving with a selection of accompaniments; for example boiled basmati rice, poppadums, sliced bananas dipped in lemon juice, lime pickle or a tomato and onion salad.

Duck à l'orange

Serves: 4
Power setting: medium or full
Total cooking time: 42–51 or 34–36 minutes

1 2kg/4½lb oven-ready duckling, trussed
salt and freshly ground black pepper
1 orange, peeled, pith removed and cut into segments
Sauce:
grated rind of 1 orange
juice of 3 oranges
15g/½oz cornflour
1 tablespoon creamed honey
To garnish:
orange slices
watercress sprigs

Prick the skin of the duck and season with salt and pepper to taste. Season and stuff the neck cavity with the orange segments. Shield the tips of the wings, tail end and legs of the duck with foil. Place in a roasting bag and stand it on a trivet or upturned saucer. Cook on medium power for 25 minutes or full power for 17 minutes. Drain and reserve the juices from the bag.

Turn the duck over and cook on medium power for a further 15–24 minutes or on full power for a further 15–17 minutes, until cooked. Remove the duck from the oven and leave to stand, wrapped in foil, for 10 minutes.

Meanwhile, to prepare the sauce, mix the orange rind, orange juice, cornflour and honey together in a jug; make up to 300ml/½pint with the reserved duck juices. Cook on full power for 2 minutes, stirring every ½ minute to keep the sauce smooth.

Serve the duck hot with the orange sauce separately. If a crisp skin is liked the duck may be placed under a preheated hot grill for a few minutes. Serve garnished with orange slices and watercress sprigs.

Casseroled pigeons in red wine

Serves: 4
Power setting: full
Total cooking time: 27 minutes

2 pigeons, cleaned and trussed
4 rashers streaky bacon, rinded
25g/1oz butter
1 tablespoon oil
1 onion, peeled and finely chopped
1 tablespoon flour
2 tablespoons redcurrant jelly
150ml/¼ pint red wine
150ml/¼ pint hot chicken stock
1 tablespoon tomato purée
salt and freshly ground black pepper
100g/4oz button mushrooms
50g/2oz stuffed green olives
2 tablespoons chopped parsley
watercress sprig to garnish

Wrap each of the pigeons in streaky bacon and secure with wooden cocktail sticks. Preheat a browning dish for 5 minutes or according to manufacturer's instructions. Add the butter, oil, and the pigeons, then cook for 4 minutes, turning to brown on all sides. Remove from the dish and reserve.

Add the onion to the dish juices, cover and cook for 2 minutes. Add the flour, blending well. Gradually add the redcurrant jelly, red wine, stock, tomato purée and salt and pepper to taste. Cook for 2 minutes, stirring half-way through the cooking time.

Return the pigeons to the dish and baste liberally with the sauce. Cover and cook for 8 minutes, stirring, and giving the dish a half-turn after 4 minutes.

Add the mushrooms, olives and parsley and cook for 6 minutes.

Allow to stand for 10 minutes before serving, garnished with watercress sprigs.

Pecan-stuffed pheasant

Serves: 2
Power setting: full and medium
Total cooking time: 25½–37½ minutes

50g/2oz butter
50g/2oz dry breadcrumbs
50g/2oz pecans, chopped
salt and freshly ground black pepper
1 1–1.5kg/2–3 lb pheasant, cleaned
150ml/¼ pint hot chicken stock
3 tablespoons sherry
To garnish:
watercress sprigs
game chips

Place half of the butter in a bowl and cook on full power for ½ minute to melt. Stir in the breadcrumbs, pecans and salt and pepper to taste. Stuff the pheasant with the pecan stuffing. Truss, and season the pheasant skin with salt and pepper to taste. Dot with the remaining butter and place in a dish. Pour over the stock and sherry. Cover the dish and cook on medium power for 20–30 minutes, giving the dish a half-turn half-way through the cooking time.

Remove the cover from the dish and cook on full power for 5–7 minutes. Allow to stand for 10–15 minutes, covered, before serving garnished with watercress sprigs and game chips.

Honeyed roast chicken with walnut stuffing

Serves: 4
Power setting: full
Total cooking time: 29½–33½ minutes

1 1.6kg/3½lb roasting chicken
Stuffing:
40g/1½oz butter or margarine

1 small onion, peeled and chopped
100g/4oz walnuts, coarsely chopped
100g/4oz fresh white breadcrumbs
grated rind of 1 lemon
2 tablespoons chopped fresh herbs
½ teaspoon ground cinnamon
salt and freshly ground black pepper
1 beaten egg or milk to mix
Baste:
2 tablespoons honey
1 teaspoon Worcestershire sauce
1 teaspoon soy sauce
To garnish:
watercress sprigs

Place the butter in a dish and cook for ½ minute to melt. Add the onion and cook for 3 minutes. Add the walnuts and cook for a further 2 minutes. Mix in the breadcrumbs, lemon rind, herbs, cinnamon, and salt and pepper to taste. Bind together with beaten egg or milk. Use to stuff the chicken.

Mix the baste ingredients together well and spread over the breast, legs and wings of the chicken. Place in a roasting bag on a roasting rack or upturned saucer and cook for 24–28 minutes, giving the dish a half-turn half-way through the cooking time. Allow to stand for 5 minutes before serving garnished with watercress sprigs.

Vegetables and salads

Guide to cooking fresh vegetables

Vegetable	Quantity	Water/salt	Preparation	Cooking time in minutes on full power	Cooking notes
Artichokes –globe	1	8 tablespoons/ ½ teaspoon	Discard the tough, outer leaves. Snip the tips off the remaining leaves and cut off the stems. Cover to cook.	5–6	To test if cooked try to pull a leaf from the whole artichoke. If it comes away freely, the artichoke is cooked. Drain upside down before serving.
	2	8 tablespoons/ ½ teaspoon		7–8	
	4	250ml/8fl oz/ 1 teaspoon		14–15	
Asparagus	450g/1lb	6 tablespoons/ ½ teaspoon	Place in a dish, arranging thicker stems to the outside of the dish and tips to the centre. Cover to cook.	12–14	Give the dish a half-turn after 6 minutes cooking time.
Aubergines	2 medium halved	2 tablespoons/ ¼ teaspoon	Cover to cook.	7–9	Scoop out the cooked flesh from the halved aubergines and use as required.
	1 whole, peeled and cubed	2 tablespoons/ ¼ teaspoon		5–6	Stir the cubed aubergine after 3 minutes cooking time.
Beans, all except thin French beans	450g/1lb	8 tablespoons/ ½ teaspoon	Cover to cook.	14–16	Stir the beans twice during cooking. Test after the minimum time to see if cooked.

Vegetable	Quantity	Water/salt	Preparation	Cooking time in minutes on full power	Cooking notes
French beans	450g/1lb	8 tablespoons/ ½ teaspoon	Cover to cook.	5–7	
Beetroot	2 medium	8 tablespoons/ ½ teaspoon	Cover to cook.	12–16	Stir or re-arrange half-way through the cooking time. Allow to stand for
	5 medium	8 tablespoons/ ½ teaspoon		22–25	10 minutes before peeling.
Broccoli	450g/1 lb	8 tablespoons/ ½ teaspoon	Place in a dish ar-ranging the stalks to the outside and florets in the centre. Cover to cook.	10–12	Stir or give the dish a half-turn after 6 minutes.
Brussels sprouts	450g/1lb	4 tablespoons/ ½ teaspoon	Trim away any damaged or coarse leaves and cut large sprouts in half. Cover to cook.	7–9	Stir the sprouts after 4 minutes cooking time.
Cabbage –shredded	450g/1lb	8 tablespoons/ ½ teaspoon	Use a large dish and ensure that the cab-bags fits loosely. Cover to cook.	8–9	Stir or re-arrange half-way through the cooking time.
–quartered	450g/1lb	8 tablespoons/ ½ teaspoon		10–12	
Carrots –whole	450g/1lb 1kg/2lb	8 tablespoons/ ½ teaspoon		12–14 18–20	Stir or re-arrange half-way through the cooking time.

Vegetable	Quantity	Water/salt	Preparation	Cooking time in minutes on full power	Cooking notes
–sliced	450g/1lb	8 tablespoons/ ½ teaspoon	Cut carrots into 1cm /½in thick slices. Cover to cook.	12–14	
Cauliflower	1 medium about 675g/1½lb	8 tablespoons/ ½ teaspoon	Cook whole cauliflower on medium high power.	13–17	Turn a whole cauliflower or florets half-way through the cooking time. Allow whole cauliflower to stand for 5 minutes after cooking.
–florets	450g/1lb	8 tablespoons/ ½ teaspoon	Cover to cook.	10–12	
Celery –whole or sliced	450g/1lb	4 tablespoons/ ¼ teaspoon	Cover to cook.	14–16	Turn or stir half-way through the cooking time.
Chicory –whole	4 medium	4 tablespoons	Cover to cook and add salt after cooking.	5–8	Re-arrange half-way through the cooking time.
Corn on the cob	1 2 4 6	3 tablespoons 3 tablespoons 5 tablespoons 5 tablespoons	Cover to cook.	4–5 7–8 13–15 17–20	Re-arrange half-way through the cooking time if cooking 4–6 cobs. Cook the corn in the husk, if liked, with no water. Dot lightly with 25g/1oz butter before cooking.
Courgettes –sliced –whole	450g/1 lb 6 small		Cover to cook.	5–6 7	Stir or re-arrange half-way through the cooking time.

Vegetable	Quantity	Water/salt	Preparation	Cooking time in minutes on full power	Cooking notes
Leeks –sliced	450g/1lb	4 tablespoons/ ½ teaspoon	Cover to cook.	10–12	Stir half-way through the cooking time.
Marrow –sliced	450g/1lb		Cover with grease-proof paper.	8–10	Stir half-way through the cooking time.
Mushrooms –whole or sliced	225g/8oz	2 tablespoons water or butter	Cover to cook. Add salt, if liked, after cooking.	2–4	Stir half-way through the cooking time.
	450g/1lb			4–6	
Onions –whole or quartered	4 medium	4 tablespoons/ ½ teaspoon	Cover to cook.	10–12	Stir half-way through the cooking time.
	8 medium			14–16	
Parsnips –cubed	450g/1lb	8 tablespoons/ ½ teaspoon	Cover to cook.	8–10	Stir half-way through the cooking time.
Peas –shelled	450g/1lb	8 tablespoons/ ½ teaspoon	Cover to cook.	9–11	Stir half-way through the cooking time. Add 15–25g/ ½–1oz butter after cooking and allow to stand for 5 minutes before serving.
	1kg/2lb			12–14	
Potatoes –peeled and quartered	450g/1lb	8 tablespoons/ ½ teaspoon	Cover to cook.	10–14	Stir twice before cooking.
–baked in skins	1		Prick thoroughly and cook on absorbent kitchen paper.	4–6	Potatoes may still feel firm when cooked. Leave to stand for 3–4 minutes to soften.
	2			6–8	
	3			8–12	
	4			12–16	

Guide to cooking frozen vegetables

Vegetable	Quantity	Cooking time in minutes on full power
Asparagus	225g/8oz	6–7
	450g/1lb	11
Beans		
–broad	225g/8oz	8
French	450g/1lb	10
or runner	225g/8oz	7
Broccoli	450g/1lb	10
	225g/8oz	6–8
Cabbage	450g/1lb	8–10
	225g/8oz	6–8
Carrots	450g/1lb	10–11
	225g/8oz	7
Cauliflower	450g/1lb	10
–florets	225g/8 oz	5
Corn	450g/1lb	8
–kernels	225g/8oz	4
–on the cob	450/1lb	7–8
	1	4–5
	2	7–8
Courgettes	225g/8oz	4
	450g/1lb	7
Diced mixed	225g/8oz	5–6
vegetables	450g/1lb	7–9
Peas	225g/8oz	4
	450g/1lb	8
Spinach		
–chopped, or leaf	225g/8oz	7–8
Root vegetable	450g/1lb	10–11
stewpack (mixed)	225g/8oz	7
Swedes	450g/1lb	10
	225g/8oz	7
Turnips	450g/1lb	11
	225g/8 oz	8
	450g/1lb	12

Blanching vegetables for the freezer

Prepare the vegetables as you would for normal cooking and place them in a covered dish, then add water as given in the chart. Cook for half the time given in the chart and stir, re-cover and cook for the remaining time, then stir again. Plunge the vegetables into iced water immediately to prevent further cooking. Drain and spread on absorbent kitchen paper to absorb excess moisture. Pack in freezer containers or boil-in-the-bag pouches, seal and label, then freeze. To pack vegetables for free-flow use, spread them on baking sheets or freezer trays and freeze until solid. Pack the frozen vegetables in bags, seal and label.

Alternatively, for extra convenience and speed, the vegetables may be blanched in boil-in-the-bags, and then, still in their bags, plunged into iced water up to their necks to cool. This chills the vegetables and expels the air in the bag at the same time, automatically creating a vacuum pack ready for freezing. Seal and label in the usual way.

Guide to blanching vegetables

Vegetable	Quantity	Water (table-spoons)	Time in minutes on full power
Asparagus	450g/1lb	3	3–4
Beans	450g/1lb	6	5–6
Broccoli	450g/1lb	6	5–6
Brussels sprouts	450g/1lb	6	5–6
Cabbage –shredded	450g/1lb	3	4–4½
Carrots –sliced	450g/1lb	3	3–4
–whole	450g/1lb	3	6–7
Cauliflower –florets	450g/1lb	6	4½–5
Corn on the cob	4	3	5–6
Courgettes –sliced	450g/1lb	3	3–3½
Leeks –sliced	450g/1lb	3	5–6
Marrow –sliced or cubed	450g/1lb	3	4–4½
Onions –quartered	4 medium	6	4–4½
Parsnips –cubed	450g/1lb	3	3–4
Peas	450g/1lb	3	4–4½
	1kg/2lb	3	6–7
Spinach	450g/1lb		3–3½
Turnips –cubed	450g/1lb	3	3–4

Guide to cooking dried beans and peas

Beans	Quantity	Preparation and cooking time
Kidney, flageolet, butter or haricot beans and chickpeas	350g/12oz	Place the beans in a large dish with a little chopped onion, celery and carrot. Add 2 teaspoons salt and pepper to taste. Cover with 1.4l/2½ pints cold stock and cook on full power for 20 minutes. Stir, re-cover and cook on medium power for 1 hour 30 minutes–1 hour 40 minutes, or until tender.
Split peas or lentils	225g/8oz	Place the split peas or lentils in a large dish with a little chopped onion, celery and 1 tablespoon lemon juice. Add a little salt and pepper to taste. Cover with 900ml/1½ pints cold stock or water. Cover and cook on full power for 15 minutes. Stir and cook on full power for a further 10 minutes or on medium power for 60–70 minutes, stirring every 30 minutes, until tender.

Green peas à la Francaise

Serves: 4
Power setting: full
Total cooking time: 5 minutes

25g/1oz butter
1 firm lettuce heart, shredded
275g/10 oz frozen peas or petits pois

salt and freshly ground pepper

Place the butter in a medium casserole and cook for 1 minute. Add the lettuce, peas and salt and pepper to taste. Cover and cook for 2 minutes. Stir well and cook, uncovered, for a further 2 minutes. Serve at once.

Peas with water chestnuts

Serves: 3
Power setting: full
Total cooking time: 6–8 minutes

225g/8 oz frozen peas
2 tablespoons water
½ teaspoon salt
½ teaspoon sugar
25g/1oz butter
1 225g/8oz can water chestnuts, drained and sliced

Place the peas in a bowl with the water, cover and cook for 5–6 minutes, stirring half-way through the cooking time.

Stir in the salt, sugar, butter and water chestnuts, cover and cook for a further 1–2 minutes. Serve at once.

Cheesy stuffed potatoes
Serves: 4
Power setting: full
Total cooking time: 15–16 minutes

4 175g/6 oz potatoes
75g/3 oz corned beef, chopped
75g/3oz Cheddar cheese, grated
50g/2oz butter
1 tablespoon tomato ketchup
1 tablespoon Worcestershire sauce
1 teaspoon dried mixed herbs
salt and freshly ground black pepper

Scrub, dry and prick the potatoes with a fork. Arrange on a double sheet of absorbent kitchen towel, spaced well apart. Cook for 6 minutes, turn over and re-arrange, then cook for a further 6–7 minutes. Leave to stand for 5 minutes then split in half and scoop out the flesh, reserving the potato skins.

Mash the potato flesh with the corned beef, 50g/2oz of the cheese, the butter, tomato ketchup, Worcestershire sauce, herbs and salt and pepper to taste. Pile back into the potato skins and sprinkle with the remaining cheese. Cook for a further 3 minutes until hot and bubbly. Brown under a preheated hot grill if liked.

French baked potatoes with cream and cheese

Serves: 4
Power setting: full
Total cooking time: 12 minutes

450g/1lb thinly sliced potatoes
200ml/7fl oz double cream
50g/2oz Cheddar cheese, grated
4 tablespoons grated Parmesan cheese
25g/1oz butter
salt and freshly ground black pepper

Place a layer of sliced potatoes in the bottom of a greased shallow dish. Top with one quarter of the cream. Mix the cheeses together and sprinkle about 2 tablespoons of the mixture over the cream. Dot with a little butter and season to taste with salt and pepper. Continue layering the ingredients in this order, finishing with a layer of grated cheese dotted with butter.

Cover with cling film, snipping two holes in the top to allow the steam to escape. Cook for 12 minutes, giving the dish a half-turn half-way through the cooking time. Allow to stand for 5 minutes before serving. Brown under a preheated hot grill if liked.

Serve with chops, steak or chicken.

Glazed carrots

Serves: 4
Power setting: full
Total cooking time: 12½–14½ minutes

450g/1lb carrots, peeled and sliced

8 tablespoons water
25g/1oz butter
50g/2oz brown sugar
salt and freshly ground black pepper
1 teaspoon Meaux mustard

Place the carrots in a dish with the water. Cover and cook for 10–12 minutes, stirring half-way through the cooking time. Drain thoroughly.

Place the butter in a bowl and cook for ½ minute to melt. Stir in the sugar, salt and pepper to taste, and mustard. Pour over the carrots and toss well to blend. Cover and cook for a further 2 minutes.

Red cabbage and apple

Serves: 4
Power setting: full
Total cooking time: 12–14 minutes

1 medium red cabbage, shredded
3 tablespoons apple juice or water
4 cooking apples, peeled, cored and sliced
pinch of ground nutmeg or ground cloves
50g/2oz butter
1 tablespoon brown sugar

Place the cabbage in a casserole with the apple juice or water and apples. Cover and cook for 12–14 minutes until tender, stirring half-way through the cooking time.

Stir in the nutmeg or cloves, butter and sugar, blending well. Serve hot with roasts, game and frankfurters.

Braised celery

Serves: 4
Power setting: full
Total cooking time: 20½–22½ minutes

50g/2oz butter
350g/12oz celery, cut into 7.5cm/3in lengths
2 rashers bacon, rinded and chopped

300ml/½ pint chicken stock
salt and freshly ground black pepper
chopped parsley to garnish

Place the butter in a shallow cooking dish and cook for 1½ minutes to melt. Add the celery and bacon, mixing well. Cook, uncovered, for 3 minutes.

Add the stock and salt and pepper to taste. Cover and cook for 16–18 minutes, giving the dish a half-turn half-way through the cooking time. Serve piping hot, sprinkled with chopped parsley.

Cauliflower cheese

Serves: 4
Power setting: medium/high
Total cooking time: 16–20 minutes

1 medium cauliflower, weighing about 675g/1½lb
8 tablespoons water
½ teaspoon salt
cheese sauce (see page 121)
25g/1oz grated cheese

Trim the head of cauliflower and place in a deep dish with the water and salt. Cover with cling film, snipping two holes in the top to allow any steam to escape. Cook for 13–17 minutes, turning over half-way through the cooking time. Allow to stand for 5 minutes then drain.

Place the cauliflower in a serving dish and pour over the cheese sauce. Sprinkle with the grated cheese and cook for 3 minutes or until the cheese melts. Brown under a preheated hot grill if liked.

Ratatouille

Serves: 4
Power setting: full
Total cooking time: 17 minutes

4 tablespoons oil
2 onions, peeled and thinly sliced
1 clove garlic, peeled and crushed
225g/8 oz courgettes, thinly sliced

350g/12oz aubergines, thinly sliced
1 green pepper, cored, seeded and sliced
225g/8 oz tomatoes, skinned and chopped
2 tablespoons chopped parsley
salt and freshly ground black pepper

Place the oil, onions and garlic in a bowl and cook for 2 minutes. Add the courgettes, aubergines and green pepper. Cover and cook for 8 minutes.

Stir in the tomatoes, parsley and salt and pepper to taste. Cover and cook for a further 7 minutes. Serve hot or cold as an appetizer or hot with meat, fish and poultry.

Stuffed tomatoes

Serves: 3
Power setting: full and medium
Total cooking time: 19–23 minutes

6 large beef tomatoes
Stuffing:
50g/2oz butter
2 onions, peeled and chopped
100g/4oz long-grain rice
1 teaspoon dried basil
salt and freshly ground pepper
200ml/7fl oz chicken stock
6 anchovy fillets, chopped

Using a serrated knife, cut off and reserve the tops of the tomatoes from the stem end. Carefully scoop out and discard the seeds but reserve and chop the pulp.

To make the stuffing, place the butter in a bowl and cook on full power for 1 minute. Add the onion, cover and cook on full power for 3 minutes. Stir in the tomato pulp, rice, basil, salt and pepper to taste, and stock. Cook, covered, on full power for 10–12 minutes, then leave to stand, covered, for 5 minutes.

Stir in the anchovy fillets and spoon equal amounts into the tomato cases. Stand in a shallow baking dish and cook on medium power for 5–7 minutes, giving the dish a half-turn once during the cooking time. Serve hot or allow to cool and serve with a mixed salad.

Crispy bacon salad with Danish Blue dressing

Serves: 4
Power setting: full
Total cooking time: 6–7 minutes

225g/8oz back bacon, rinds removed
¼ cucumber, cut into fine julienne strips
1 red pepper, cored, seeded and sliced
1 green pepper, cored, seeded and sliced
225g/8oz beansprouts
2 small oranges, peeled, pith removed, and cut into segments
½ crisp lettuce, shredded
Danish Blue dressing:
50g/2oz Danish Blue cheese
150ml/¼ pint natural yoghurt
2 tablespoons white wine vinegar
1 tablespoon grated onion or snipped chives
freshly ground black pepper

Place the bacon on a bacon rack or plate and cover with absorbent kitchen towel. Cook for 6–7 minutes until crisp. Allow to cool.

Crumble or cut the bacon into strips. Mix with the cucumber, red pepper, green pepper, beansprouts and orange segments.

Line a serving dish with the shredded lettuce and pile the bacon salad mixture into the centre.

Meanwhile, mash the cheese with a fork to soften. Gradually add the yoghurt, beating well to blend. Stir in the vinegar, onion or chives, and pepper to taste. Chill before serving with the crispy bacon salad.

Summer orange potato salad

Serves: 4–6
Power setting: full
Total cooking time: 16–18 minutes

900g/2lb new potatoes, scrubbed and diced
8 tablespoons water
4 oranges
4 tablespoons mayonnaise
1 tablespoon snipped chives
salt and freshly ground black pepper

Place the potatoes and water in a large shallow dish. Cover with cling film, snipping two holes in the top to allow the steam to escape. Cook for 16–18 minutes, shaking the dish vigorously twice during the cooking time. Leave to stand for 3 minutes, then drain through a fine sieve.

Meanwhile, finely grate the rind from two of the oranges and mix with the mayonnaise, chives and salt and pepper to taste.

Peel the oranges, removing all the pith and slice into segments. Mix with the potatoes and mayonnaise mixture, tossing gently to coat. Serve hot or cold.

Marinated mushroom salad

Serves: 4
Power setting: full
Total cooking time: 3½–4 minutes

100g/4oz back bacon, rinds removed
350g/12oz button mushrooms, sliced
Dressing:
4 tablespoons soured cream
3 tablespoons horseradish mustard
1 tablespoon lemon juice
4 tablespoons oil
2 tablespoons milk
salt and freshly ground black pepper

Place the bacon on a bacon rack or plate and cover with absorbent kitchen towel. Cook for 3½–4 minutes until crisp. Allow to cool.

Place the mushrooms in a serving bowl. Mix all the dressing ingredients together with salt and pepper to taste until smooth and creamy. Spoon over the mushrooms and toss carefully.

Crumble or cut the bacon into strips and sprinkle over the mushroom salad when ready to serve.

Italian salad

Serves: 4
Power setting: full

Total cooking time: 3–4 minutes

225g/8 oz green beans, topped and tailed
4 tablespoons water
225g/8 oz courgettes, thinly sliced
4 tomatoes, cut into wedges
Dressing:
2 tablespoons tarragon and thyme mustard
4 tablespoons oil
1 teaspoon sugar
1 teaspoon lemon juice
salt and freshly ground black pepper

Place the beans in a bowl with the water. Cover and cook for 3–4 minutes, stirring half-way through the cooking time. Drain, leave to cool then cut into bite-sized pieces.

Mix the beans, courgettes and tomatoes in a salad bowl. Mix all the dressing ingredients together with salt and pepper to taste. Pour over the salad and toss gently to mix. Serve at once.

Egg and cheese dishes

Fried eggs

Use a flat-based microwave browning dish. Preheat the dish
according to the manufacturer's instructions – about 1 minute for
each egg on full power. Melt 1 teaspoon butter on the dish per egg
being cooked and break the eggs into the dish. Cover and cook for the
times given below:

Eggs	Cooking time in seconds/ minutes on medium power	Cooking time in seconds/ minutes on full power
1	45–55 seconds	40–50 seconds
2	1½–2 minutes	1½–1¾ minutes
4	2–2½ minutes	2–¼ minutes

Poached eggs

Use small dishes or cocottes or use a large dish. If you are using small
dishes, pour 6 tablespoons hot water into each with a dash of vinegar.
Bring to the boil on full power for about 1½ minutes. Carefully break
the egg into the dish and prick the yolk quickly with the tip of a
pointed knife. Cook for the times given below.

Alternatively, place 475ml/16 fl oz hot water in a large dish and
bring to the boil by cooking on full power for 5–6 minutes. Break the
eggs on to a plate and quickly prick the yolks with the tip of a pointed
knife. Swirl the water with a spoon and slip the eggs gently into it.
Cook on medium power for the times given below. Allow to stand in
the cooking water for ½–1 minute before removing with a slotted
spoon to serve.

Eggs	Cooking time in minutes on medium power	Cooking time in minutes on full power
1	1	¾–1
2	1¾	1–1½
3	2½	1½–2½
4	3¼	2½–3

Scrambled eggs

Eggs	Butter	Milk power	Cooking time in minutes on full
1	1 teaspoon	1 tablespoon	¾–1
2	2 teaspoons	2 tablespoons	1¾–2
4	4 teaspoons	4 tablespoons	3¾–4
6	2 tablespoons	6 tablespoons	5½–6

Break the eggs into a dish, add the milk and salt and pepper to taste and beat together with a fork until light. Add the butter and cook for half the recommended time. Stir the set pieces of egg from the outside of the dish to the centre, then cook for the remaining recommended time, stirring twice. When cooked, the eggs should just be beginning to set. Allow to stand for 1–2 minutes for the eggs to complete cooking and become lightly set with any residual heat. Stir gently before serving.

Boiled eggs

Until recently it was thought impossible to cook boiled eggs in the microwave oven. The pressure created within the shell during cooking caused the eggs to explode. After various tests to find a method for cooking boiled eggs the following method has been found to work satisfactorily.

Wrap an egg in a piece of foil (small amounts of foil are permissible for use in the microwave) and place in a small cup of boiling water. Cook in the microwave for 5 minutes. Remove the egg from the foil and serve. The egg will be lightly boiled with a runny yolk.

Plain omelette

Serves: 2
Power setting: full

Total cooking time: 3¾–4 minutes

4 eggs, beaten
3 tablespoons milk
½ teaspoon salt
freshly ground black pepper
15g/½oz butter

Mix the eggs with the milk, salt and pepper to taste, blending well.

Place the butter in a 25cm/10in pie plate and cook for ½ minute to melt. Brush the butter over the plate to coat. Pour in the egg mixture, cover with cling film, snipping two holes in the top to allow any steam to escape, and cook for 1½ minutes. Using a fork, move the cooked egg from the edge of the dish to the centre. Re-cover and cook for a further 1¼–1½ minutes, then allow to stand for 1½–2 minutes to finish cooking. Loosen the omelette with a spatula and fold in half to serve.

Variations

Bacon omelette: Coarsely chop 3 rashers of rindless bacon. Place in a bowl and cook for 2–3 minutes until crisp and brown. Allow to cool then crumble into the egg mixture. Prepare and cook as above. *Total cooking time*: 5¼–6½ minutes

Cheese omelette: Sprinkle the omelette with 50g/2oz grated Cheddar cheese before leaving to stand. Fold the omelette in half and cook for a further ½ minute. *Total cooking time*: 4¼–4½ minutes.

Spanish omelette: Place 1 finely chopped onion, 1 finely chopped green pepper and 1 chopped tomato in a bowl with 25g/1oz butter. Cover and cook for 3 minutes. Mix with 1 large cooked and diced potato. Add to the omelette mixture before cooking. Prepare and cook as above allowing an extra ½–1 minute cooking time if necessary. *Total cooking time*: 6¾–7½ minutes.

Stilton baked eggs

Serves: 4
Power setting: full
Total cooking time: 3 minutes

1 170g/6oz packet frozen chopped spinach, thawed and drained
100g/4 oz Stilton cheese, grated
4 eggs
ground nutmeg

Divide the spinach between four small ramekins. Reserve a little of the cheese and sprinkle the rest on top of the spinach. Break an egg into each dish and sprinkle with a little ground nutmeg. Sprinkle the remaining Stilton cheese over the eggs.

Cook, two at a time, for 1½ minutes, giving the dishes a half-turn half-way through the cooking time. Serve hot with crisp toast as a starter.

Spaghetti and bacon omelette

Serves: 2
Power setting: full
Total cooking time: 8¼–9½ minutes

2 rashers rindless bacon, chopped
1 425g/15oz can spaghetti in tomato sauce
4 eggs, beaten
3 tablespoons milk
½ teaspoon salt
freshly ground black pepper
15g/½oz butter

Place the bacon in a bowl and cook for 2–3 minutes until crisp and brown. Drain on absorbent kitchen towel.

Place the spaghetti in a bowl and cook for 3 minutes, stirring after 2 minutes.

Meanwhile, mix the eggs, milk, salt and pepper to taste until well blended. Place the butter in a 25cm/10in pie plate and cook for ½ minute to melt. Brush the melted butter over the plate and pour in the egg mixture. Cover with cling film, snipping two holes in the top to allow the steam to escape. Cook for 1½ minutes, then, using a fork or spatula, move the cooked egg from the edge of the dish to the centre. Re-cover and cook for 1¼–1½ minutes, then allow to stand for 1½–2 minutes. Loosen the omelette, spread one half with the hot spaghetti and fold the other half over. Divide into two portions and serve immediately, sprinkled with the bacon pieces.

Cheese fondue

Serves: 4
Power setting: full and medium
Total cooking time: 7–8 minutes

250ml/8fl oz dry white wine or cider
2 tablespoons Kirsch (optional)
275g/10oz Gruyère cheese, grated
275g/10oz Emmenthal cheese, grated
3 tablespoons plain flour
freshly ground black pepper
To serve:
cubes of French bread

Place the wine or cider and Kirsch, if used, in a fondue dish or deep dish. Cook on full power for 4 minutes or until very hot.

Toss the cheeses with the flour and pepper to taste until evenly coated. Quickly stir or whisk into the wine and cover the dish. Cook, on medium power for 3–4 minutes, stirring every minute, until the cheese has melted and the mixture is smooth and creamy. Serve at once with cubes of French bread for dipping.

Microwave cheesy pizzas

Serves: 4
Power setting: full
Total cooking time: 7 minutes

4 15cm/6in ready-baked pizza bases
1 large onion, peeled and chopped
2 cloves garlic, peeled and crushed
1 tablespoon oil
150g/5oz tomato purée
50g/2oz canned anchovies
2 tablespoons capers
100g/4oz black olives
350g/12 oz Mozzarella cheese, grated

Place the pizza bases on a large baking sheet. Place the onion, garlic and oil in a bowl and cook for 2 minutes. Stir in the tomato purée and cook for 1 minute. Spread equal amounts of the mixture on each pizza, top with a few anchovies, capers and black olives. Cover with grated cheese then decorate each pizza with the remaining anchovies, capers and black olives.

Cook for 4 minutes, giving the dish a half-turn half-way through the cooking time. Serve hot with a crisp green salad.

Cheese soufflé

Serves: 6
Power setting: full, low and medium
Total cooking time: 27–32 minutes

25g/1oz plain flour
¾ teaspoon salt
½ teaspoon mustard powder
pinch of ground paprika
2 170g/6oz cans evaporated milk
225g/8oz strong Cheddar cheese, grated
6 eggs, separated
1 teaspoon cream of tartar

It is possible to cook a soufflé in the microwave oven but because of the speed of cooking it is necessary to stabilize the mixture. For success it is necessary to use evaporated milk in the base sauce. It is important to remember, however, that a microwave soufflé does not form a crust and rises very high, so it requires a larger dish than conventionally baked soufflés of similar quantities.

Place the flour, salt, mustard powder and paprika in a bowl. Blend in the evaporated milk and cook on full power for 4–6 minutes, stirring every 2 minutes until thickened. Add the cheese and stir well to mix. Cook on full power for 1–2 minutes until melted.

Whisk the egg whites with the cream of tartar until they stand in stiff peaks. Beat the egg yolks separately until pale and creamy. Pour the cheese sauce over the egg yolks and mix well to blend. Add the egg whites and fold in gently until well combined.

Pour the mixture into an ungreased 2.25l/4pint soufflé dish. Cook on low power for 10 minutes, then on medium power for 12–14 minutes, giving the dish a quarter-turn every 5 minutes, or until the top edges appear dry and the soufflé has a set appearance. Serve at once.

Rice, pasta and cereals

Guide to cooking rice and pasta

Rice	Quantity	Preparation	Cooking time in minutes on full power	Standing time
Brown rice	225g/8oz	Place in a deep, covered container with 600 ml/1 pint boiling salted water.	20–25	5–10
American easy-cook rice	225g/8oz	Place in a deep, covered container with 600ml/1 pint boiling salted water.	12	5–10
Long-grain patna rice	225/8oz	Place in a deep, covered container with 600ml/1 pint boiling salted water and 1 tablespoon oil.	10	5–10

Pasta	Quantity	Preparation	Cooking time in minutes on full power	Standing time
Egg noodles and tagliatelle	225g/8oz	Place in a deep, covered container with 600 ml/1 pint boiling salted water and 1 tablespoon oil.	6	3
Macaroni	225g/8oz	Place in a deep, covered container with 600ml/1 pint boiling salted water and 1 tablespoon oil.	10	3
Pasta shells and shapes	225g/8oz	Place in a deep, covered container with 900ml/1½ pints salted water and 1 tablespoon oil.	12–14	5–10
Spaghetti	225g/8oz	Hold in a deep, covered container with 1 l/1¾ pints boiling salted water to soften, then submerge or break in half and add 1 tablespoon oil.	12	5–10

Prawn and mussel paella

Serves: 4
Power setting: full
Total cooking time: 21 minutes

1 small onion, peeled and finely chopped
½ green pepper, cored, seeded and chopped
1 tablespoon oil
225g/8oz long-grain rice
600ml/1 pint hot chicken stock
2 tablespoons chopped fresh parsley
1 tablespoon snipped chives
salt and freshly ground black pepper
2 150g/5oz cans mussels in brine, drained
225g/8oz peeled prawns
3 tomatoes, peeled, seeded and chopped

Place the onion, pepper and oil in a medium-sized dish and cook for 5 minutes, stirring half-way through the cooking time. Add the rice, chicken stock, parsley, chives and salt and pepper to taste. Cover and cook for 10 minutes, stirring half-way through the cooking time.

Add the mussels, prawns and tomatoes, blending well. Cover and cook for a further 6 minutes. Serve at once.

Turkey risotto

Serves: 3–4
Power setting: full
Total cooking time: 20–25½ minutes

50g/2oz butter
175g/6 oz chopped onion
100g/4oz chopped green pepper
1 large stalk celery, chopped
225g/8 oz long-grain rice
600ml/1 pint boiling chicken stock
salt and freshly ground black pepper
2 tablespoons raisins
225g/8oz cooked turkey, cut into bite-sized pieces
4 fresh or canned pineapple slices, chopped

Place the butter in a large dish and cook for 1½ minutes. Add the onion, pepper and celery and cook for 2 minutes. Stir in the rice, stock, salt and pepper to taste, and raisins. Cover and cook for 15–20 minutes or until almost all of the stock has been absorbed by the rice.

Stir in the turkey and pineapple and cook for 2 minutes. Leave to stand, covered, for 10 minutes before serving.

Spaghetti bolognese

Serves: 4
Power setting: full
Total cooking time: 32 minutes

225g/8 oz spaghetti
1 l/1¾ pints boiling water
1 tablespoon oil
Bolognese sauce:
450g/1lb minced beef
1 onion, peeled and finely chopped
1 clove garlic, peeled and crushed
1 green pepper, cored, seeded and chopped
2 tablespoons tomato purée
450g/1 lb canned tomatoes
1 beef stock cube
2 teaspoons Worcestershire sauce
2 teaspoons dried oregano
salt and freshly ground black pepper

Hold the spaghetti in a deep, covered container with the water to soften. Submerge slowly then add the oil. Cook for 12 minutes, stirring half-way through the cooking time. Leave to stand while preparing the sauce.

Place the beef, onion, garlic and green pepper in a bowl and cook for 5 minutes, stirring after 3 minutes. Add the tomato purée and crushed canned tomatoes. Crumble in the stock cube and add the Worcestershire sauce, oregano and seasoning to taste, blending well. Cover and cook for 15 minutes, stirring every 5 minutes. Serve with the drained spaghetti.

Chicken liver cannelloni

Serves: 4
Power setting: full
Total cooking time: 19–20 minutes

8 tubes cannelloni
600ml/1 pint boiling water
1 tablespoon oil
Stuffing:
50g/2oz butter
100g/4oz mushrooms, chopped
175g/6oz chicken livers, chopped
2 cloves garlic, peeled and crushed
1 178g/6¼oz can pimentos, drained and chopped
1 225g/8 oz can peeled tomatoes, chopped
Cheese sauce (see page 121)
Parmesan cheese to sprinkle

Place the cannelloni in a dish with the water and oil. Cover and cook for 10 minutes, making sure that the cannelloni is immersed in the water. Allow to stand while making the stuffing.

Place the butter in a bowl and cook for 1 minute to melt. Add the mushrooms, chicken livers and garlic and cook for 5–6 minutes or until cooked, stirring half-way through the cooking time. Add the pimentos and tomatoes and cook for a further 2 minutes.

Drain the cannelloni and stuff each tube with the mixture using a teaspoon. Place in a serving dish and cover with the hot cheese sauce. Sprinkle with Parmesan cheese and cook for 1 minute until hot.

Macaroni cheese

Serves: 4
Power setting: full
Total cooking time: 26 minutes

225g/8oz macaroni
600 ml/1 pint boiling water
1 tablespoon oil
50g/2oz butter
1 large onion, peeled and finely chopped
25g/1oz flour

600 ml/1 pint milk
175g/6oz strong Cheddar cheese, grated
salt and freshly ground black pepper
ground paprika
To garnish:
2 tomatoes, sliced
parsley sprigs

Place the macaroni in a large bowl with the water and oil. Cover and cook for 10 minutes then allow to stand while making the sauce.

Place the butter in a bowl and cook for 1 minute to melt. Add the onion and cook for 6 minutes, stirring half-way through the cooking time. Stir in the flour and gradually add the milk. Add the cheese and cook for 5 minutes, stirring twice during the cooking time to keep the sauce smooth.

Drain the macaroni and add to the cheese mixture with salt and pepper to taste. Cook for a further 4 minutes, stirring every minute. Sprinkle with paprika and garnish with tomato slices and parsley sprigs before serving.

Noodles with bean and bacon sauce

Serves: 4
Power setting: full
Total cooking time: 10½–12½ or 13½–15½ minutes

350g/12 oz fresh or dried green noodles
900 ml/1½ pints boiling water
salt and freshly ground black pepper
2 tablespoons olive oil
4 spring onions, chopped
4 rashers lean back bacon, rinded and cut into strips
1 clove garlic, peeled and crushed
1 450g/16 oz can baked beans in tomato sauce
grated Parmesan cheese to serve

Place the pasta in a deep bowl with the boiling water, a little salt and 1 teaspoon of the oil. Cover with cling film, snipping two holes in the top to allow the steam to escape. Cook dried pasta for 6 minutes or fresh pasta for 3 minutes. Allow to stand for 3 minutes then drain.

Meanwhile, place the remaining oil in a bowl and cook for ½

minute. Add the spring onions, bacon and garlic. Cover and cook for 4 minutes. Stir in the beans and cook for 4–6 minutes until very hot and bubbly, stirring half-way through the cooking time.

Pile the drained pasta on to a serving dish. Top with the hot bean and bacon sauce. Sprinkle with Parmesan cheese and serve at once.

Curried pasta with prawns

Serves: 4
Power setting: full
Total cooking time: 23–31 minutes

225g/8 oz dried shell pasta
900ml/1½ pints boiling water
salt
4 teaspoons olive oil
2 225g/8 oz cans curried beans with sultanas
150ml/¼ pint single cream
100g/4oz peeled prawns
75g/3oz button mushrooms, thinly sliced
2 tablespoons chopped fresh parsley

Place the pasta in a deep bowl with the boiling water, a little salt and 1 teaspoon of the oil. Cover with cling film, snipping two holes in the top to allow the steam to escape. Cook for 12–14 minutes then allow to stand for 5–10 minutes.

Meanwhile, place the beans, cream, prawns, mushrooms and parsley in a bowl and cook for 6–7 minutes until hot and bubbly, stirring half-way through the cooking time.

Drain the pasta and pile on to a serving dish. Top with the hot curried bean and prawn sauce and serve at once.

Porridge

There are two main types of porridge oats – the traditional type and the quick-cooking type. Both should be cooked in a mixture of milk and water or plain water for good results. Always cook in a deep bowl – a deep individual cereal bowl is ideal for single portions and the advantage here is that you can cook and serve in the same dish (saving on washing up and reducing the risks of rapid cooling). For the best results, three-quarters cover the bowl with cling film – this enables you to stir the porridge without removing the cover. Follow the chart below for specific quantities and times, remembering that if you like a softer porridge you should leave the dish to stand for 2–3 minutes before serving:

Number of servings	Water	Salt	Cereal	Cooking times full power	in minutes low power
Traditional or slow-cook oatmeal					
1	175ml/6fl oz	¼ tsp	30g/1¼oz	3–5	10
2	350ml/12fl oz	½ tsp	65g/2½oz	6–7	10
4	750ml/1¼ pints	¾ tsp	125g/4½oz	8–9	12
Quick-cook oatmeal					
1	175ml/6fl oz	¼ tsp	30g/1¼oz	1–2	5
2	350ml/12 fl oz	½ tsp	65g/2½ oz	2–3	5
4	750ml/1¼ pints	¾ tsp	125g/4½oz	5–6	7–8

Honeyed muesli

Serves: 6–8
Power setting: full
Total cooking time: 3½ minutes

2 tablespoons clear honey
1 tablespoon sunflower oil
100g/4oz rolled oats
2 tablespoons wheatgerm
25g/1oz pine nuts, chopped
25g/1oz dried apricots or prunes, chopped
25g/1oz flaked almonds
25g/1oz dried figs, chopped
25g/1 oz sultanas

Place the honey and oil in a large bowl and cook for ½ minute. Add the oats, wheatgerm and pine nuts, mixing well to blend. Spread on to a shallow microwave baking sheet or large flat plate and cook for 3 minutes, stirring every ½ minute to ensure that the muesli browns evenly. Add the apricots or prunes, almonds, figs and sultanas, mixing well and leave to stand, covered, for 1 minute. Serve with milk, yoghurt or cream, and with fresh fruit if liked. Strawberries and bananas make good accompaniments.

Sauces, stuffings and glazes

Basic white pouring sauce

Makes: 300ml/½ pint
Power setting: full
Total cooking time: 4½–5 minutes

25g/1 oz butter
25g/1 oz plain flour
300 ml/½ pint milk
salt and freshly ground pepper

Place the butter in a large jug and cook for 1 minute to melt. Add the flour, mixing well, then gradually add the milk and salt and pepper to taste. Cook for 3½–4 minutes, stirring every minute until the sauce is smooth and thickened. Check the seasoning and use as required.

Variations

Basic white coating sauce: Prepare and cook as above but increase both the butter and flour to 50g/2oz.

Cheese sauce: Prepare and cook as above but add 50g/2oz grated cheese and a pinch of mustard powder to the sauce for the last 2 minutes cooking time, blending well.

Parsley sauce: Prepare and cook as above but add 2–3 teaspoons chopped fresh parsley to the sauce for the last 2 minutes cooking time, blending well.

Onion sauce: Place 15g/½oz butter in a bowl with 2 peeled and chopped onions. Cook on full power for 2 minutes. Add to the basic white sauce for the last 2 minutes cooking time, blending well. *Total cooking time*: 6½–7 minutes.

Prawn sauce: Add 75g/3oz peeled prawns, ½ teaspoon mustard powder, 2 teaspoons lemon juice and ¼ teaspoon anchovy essence to the sauce for the last 2 minutes cooking time, blending well.

Mushroom sauce: Place 15g/½oz butter in a bowl with 75g/3oz sliced button mushrooms. Cook on full power for 2 minutes. Drain and add to the basic white pouring sauce for the last 2 minutes cooking time, blending well. *Total cooking time*: 6½–7 minutes.

Béchamel sauce

Makes: 300ml/½ pint
Power setting: full and defrost
Total cooking time: 12½–14 minutes

1 small onion, peeled
1 carrot, peeled and sliced
1 bay leaf
blade of mace
12 peppercorns
few sprigs of parsley
300ml/½ pint milk
25g/1oz butter
25g/1oz plain flour
salt and freshly ground pepper

Place the onion, carrot, bay leaf, mace, peppercorns, parsley and milk in a large jug. Cook on defrost power for 10–11 minutes until hot.

Place the butter in another jug and cook on full power for 1 minute. Stir in the flour and salt and pepper to taste. Gradually add the strained milk, stirring continuously, and cook on full power for 1½–2 minutes until smooth and thick. Use as required.

Variations

Mornay sauce: Prepare and cook as above but add 1 egg yolk, mixed with 2 tablespoons double cream and 50g/2oz grated cheese to the hot sauce. Whisk until the cheese melts and the sauce is smooth.

Chaud-froid sauce: Prepare and cook as above. Dissolve 1 tablespoon powdered gelatine in 150ml/¼ pint hot water. Cook on full power for 1 minute then stir into the hot sauce. Use when cold and almost at setting point. *Total cooking time*: 13½–15 minutes.

Béarnaise sauce

Makes: about 100ml/4 fl oz
Power setting: full
Total cooking time: 1–1½ minutes

100g/4oz butter

4 egg yolks
1 teaspoon finely grated onion
1 teaspoon tarragon vinegar
1 teaspoon dry white wine

Place the butter in a jug and cook for 1–1½ minutes until hot and bubbly. Place the egg yolks, onion, vinegar and wine in a blender. Turn on to the highest setting and add the hot butter in a steady stream, blending until the sauce is creamy and thickened.

Serve with steaks, poached eggs on toast or cooked green vegetables.

Bread sauce

Makes: about 450ml/¾ pint
Power setting: full
Total cooking time: 6½ minutes

1 onion, peeled
6 cloves
300ml/½ pint milk
pinch of ground nutmeg
75g/3oz fresh white breadcrumbs
25g/1oz butter
1 tablespoon whipping cream
salt and freshly ground black pepper

Stud the onion with the cloves and place in a deep dish with the milk and nutmeg. Cook, uncovered, for 4 minutes.

Remove the onion and add the breadcrumbs. Cook, uncovered for 2 minutes. Add the butter and cream and mix well to blend. Cook for a further ½ minute. Season with salt and pepper to taste. Serve hot with game and poultry.

Apple sauce

Makes: 300ml/½ pint
Power setting: full
Total cooking time: 6–8 minutes

450g/1lb cooking apples, peeled, cored and sliced

15g/½oz butter
1 teaspoon lemon juice
2–3 teaspoons castor sugar
1 tablespoon water

Place the apples, butter, lemon juice, sugar and water in a bowl. Cover with cling film, snipping two holes in the top to allow the steam to escape, and cook for 6–8 minutes until soft and tender.

Beat with a spoon until smooth or purée until smooth in a blender, or pass through a fine sieve.

Serve hot with pork, duck, goose or game.

Gravy

Makes: 300ml/½ pint
Power setting: full
Total cooking time: 5–6 minutes

2 tablespoons roasting meat pan juices or drippings
1–2 tablespoons flour
300ml/½ pint hot beef or chicken stock
salt and freshly ground black pepper

Place the pan juices or drippings in a bowl and stir in sufficient flour, depending on thickness of gravy required. Cook for 3 minutes until the flour turns golden.

Gradually add the stock, blending well. Cook for 2–3 minutes, stirring every minute, until smooth and boiling. Season to taste with salt and pepper, and serve.

Hollandaise sauce

Serves: 4
Power setting: full and medium
Total cooking time: 2½ minutes

100g/4oz butter
juice of 1 medium lemon
½ teaspoon mustard powder
2 egg yolks
salt and freshly ground pepper

Place the butter in a large jug and cook on full power for 1½ minutes. Mix the lemon juice with the mustard and egg yolks and whisk into the hot butter. Whisk well to blend smoothly, then season to taste. Cook on medium power for 1 minute, taking care to ensure the sauce does not boil. Whisk briefly and adjust seasoning to taste.

Serve hot with poached salmon, globe artichokes or cooked vegetables.

Barbecue sauce

Makes: 300ml/ pint
Power setting: full
Total cooking time: 11 minutes

25g/1oz butter
2 medium onions, peeled and finely chopped
200ml/7fl oz tomato ketchup
2 tablespoons vinegar
1 tablespoon Worcestershire sauce
3 tablespoons water
1 tablespoon brown sugar
2 teaspoons lemon juice
pinch of mustard powder
salt and freshly ground black pepper

Place the butter and onions in a medium-sized bowl and cook for 3 minutes until soft and translucent. Add the remaining ingredients with salt and pepper to taste, mixing well to blend. Cover and cook for 8 minutes, stirring half-way through the cooking time.

Serve with sausages, hamburgers, barbecued chicken and spare ribs.

Tomato sauce

Makes: 450ml/¾ pint
Power setting: full
Total cooking time: 7½ minutes

25g/1oz butter
1 small onion, peeled and chopped
25g/1oz flour

1 396g/14oz can peeled tomatoes *or* 450g/1 lb fresh tomatoes, peeled, seeded
   and chopped
½ teaspoon dried basil
½ teaspoon dried oregano
150ml/¼ pint dry red wine
2 tablespoons tomato purée
1 tablespoon chopped fresh parsley
salt and freshly ground black pepper

Place the butter and onion in a large bowl. Cook for 2 minutes until
the onion is soft and translucent. Stir in the flour and cook for a further
½ minute. Gradually add the remaining ingredients with salt and
pepper to taste. Cook for 5 minutes, stirring half-way through the
cooking time.

   Serve as it is for a chunky sauce, or blend in a liquidizer until
smooth.

Sweet and sour sauce

Makes: 750ml/1¼ pints
Power setting: full
Total cooking time: 6–8 minutes

1 400g/14oz can pineapple pieces in natural juice
150ml/¼ pint chicken stock
1½ tablespoons brown sugar
3 tablespoons vinegar
2 teaspoons soy sauce
1 teaspoon tomato ketchup
1½ tablespoons cornflour
50g/2oz spring onions, trimmed and chopped
1 green pepper, cored, seeded and chopped

Drain the juices from the pineapple into a medium-sized bowl. Add
the stock, sugar, vinegar, soy sauce, tomato ketchup and cornflour,
mixing well to blend. Cook for 5–7 minutes, stirring every 2 minutes,
until clear and thickened.

   Add the pineapple, spring onions and green pepper and cook for a
further minute. Allow to stand for 5 minutes to let the flavours
develop before serving.

   Serve with shrimp, pork and chicken dishes.

Cranberry sauce

Makes: 750–900 ml/1¼–1½ pints
Power setting: full
Total cooking time: 18–20 minutes

450g/1lb fresh cranberries
6 tablespoons cold water
350g/12oz sugar

Place the cranberries, water and sugar in a large bowl. Cover with cling film, snipping two holes in the top to allow the steam to escape. Cook for 18–20 minutes, stirring every 6 minutes, until pulpy. Serve warm or cold.

Variation

Cranberry and orange sauce: Prepare and cook as above but add the finely grated rind of 1 large orange to the ingredients before cooking.

Custard sauce

Makes: 300ml/½ pint
Power setting: full
Total cooking time: 7 minutes

300ml/½ pint milk
2 eggs
1 tablespoon castor sugar
2–3 drops vanilla essence

Place the milk in a jug and cook for about 3 minutes or until almost boiling. Lightly beat the eggs, sugar and vanilla essence together. Pour the milk on to this mixture, stir well to blend and strain back into the jug.

Return to the microwave in a water bath containing hand-hot water and cook for 4 minutes, stirring every minute to keep the sauce smooth. The custard is cooked when it lightly coats the back of the spoon.

Variation

Simple custard sauce: In a large jug mix 1–2 tablespoons sugar with 1 tablespoon custard powder and a little milk from 300 ml/½ pint, gradually blend in the remaining milk and cook for 3–4 minutes until smooth and thick, stirring or whisking every minute. Add 2–3 drops of vanilla essence before serving. *Total cooking time*: 3–4 minutes.

Hot cherry sauce

Makes: 450ml/¾ pint
Power setting: full
Total cooking time: 5 minutes

1 425g/15oz can stoned black cherries
1 tablespoon cornflour
1½ teaspoons lemon juice
1 teaspoon grated lemon rind

Drain the syrup or juice from the cherries into a medium-sized bowl. Add the cornflour, mixing well to blend. Cook, uncovered, for 4 minutes, stirring every minute, until the sauce is smooth and thickened.

Add the cherries, lemon juice and lemon rind, blending well. Cook for 1 minute until hot.

Serve hot over ice cream or nut sundaes.

Speedy chocolate sauce

Serves: 4–6
Power setting: full
Total cooking time: 4–6 minutes

75g/3 oz white sugar
75g/3oz soft brown sugar
75g/3oz cocoa powder
300ml/½ pint milk
1 teaspoon vanilla essence
25g/1oz butter

Place the sugars, cocoa, milk, vanilla essence and butter in a bowl, blending well. Cook for 4–6 minutes, stirring every minute, until smooth and thickened. The sauce will coat the back of a wooden spoon when cooked.

Serve warm or cold with ice cream, profiteroles and baked or steamed puddings.

Festive stuffing

Makes: 12 stuffing balls
Power setting: full
Total cooking time: 10 minutes

450g/1lb pork sausagemeat
100g/4oz cooked ham, finely chopped
1 onion, peeled and grated
1 dessert apple, peeled, cored and finely chopped
1 teaspoon dried mixed herbs
25g/1oz fresh white breadcrumbs
salt and freshly ground black pepper

Mix the sausagemeat with the ham, onion, apple, mixed herbs, breadcrumbs and salt and pepper to taste, blending well.

Divide the mixture into 12 portions and shape each into a ball. Cook in two batches, for 5 minutes each, in a microwave bun tray, or place all on a large plate or roasting rack and cook for 10 minutes, giving the dish a half-turn half-way through the cooking time. Allow to stand for 5 minutes before serving.

Lemon, apple and sage stuffing

Makes: enough to stuff 1 large chicken
Power setting: full
Total cooking time: 5 minutes

25g/1oz butter
1 small onion, peeled and chopped
1 dessert apple, cored and finely chopped
1 chicken liver, chopped
1 tablespoon chopped fresh sage

grated rind of 1 lemon
50g/2oz fresh white or brown breadcrumbs
salt and freshly ground black pepper
1 egg, beaten

Place the butter in a bowl and cook for 1 minute to melt. Add the onion, apple and liver, cover and cook for 4 minutes. Add the sage, lemon rind, breadcrumbs and salt and pepper to taste. Bind together with some of the beaten egg. Use as required.

Honey and marmalade glaze

Makes: 120ml/4½fl oz
Power setting: full
Total cooking time: 1–1½ minutes

2 tablespoons clear honey
6 tablespoons orange or lemon marmalade

Place the honey and marmalade in a small dish and cook for 1–1½ minutes until hot and syrupy.

Use to baste and glaze cooked ham, gammon steaks and chicken.

Puddings and desserts

Guide to cooking fruit

Fruit–type and quantity	Preparation	Cooking time in minutes on full power
450g/1lb apricots	Stone and wash, then sprinkle with 100g/4oz sugar.	6–8
450g/1lb cooking apples	Peel, core and slice, then sprinkle with 100g/4oz sugar.	6–8
450g/1lb gooseberries	Top and tail, then sprinkle with 100g/4oz sugar.	4
4 medium-sized sized peaches	Stone and wash, then sprinkle with 100g/4oz sugar	4–5
6 medium-sized pears	Peel, halve and core. Dissolve 75g/3oz sugar in a little water and pour over the pears.	8–10
450g/1lb plums, cherries, damsons or greengages	Stone and wash. Sprinkle with 100g/4oz the grated rind of ½ lemon.	4–5
450g/1lb soft berry fruits	Top and tail or hull. Wash and add 100g/4oz sugar.	3–5
450g/1lb rhubarb	Trim and cut into short lengths. Add 100g/4oz sugar and the grated rind of 1 lemon	8–10

Guide to defrosting fruit

Defrost fruits in their covered freezer containers, if suitable, for the times given below, or transfer the fruit to a suitable covered dish first. The times given will partially defrost the fruit; it should then be allowed to stand at room temperature to thaw completely by means of the residual heat. The times given are approximate and will depend upon the freezing method used, the type und shape of the container and the variety of the fruit. During defrosting gently shake or stir the contents to ensure even heat distribution.

Quantity of fruit and freezing methods	Time in minutes on full power	Time in minutes on defrost power
450g/1lb fruit, dry packed with sugar	4–8	
450g/1lb fruit packed with sugar syrup	8–12	
450g/1lb free-flow fruit (open frozen)		4–8

Fruit crumble

Serves: 4
Power setting: full
Total cooking time: 11–13 minutes

450g/1lb fresh, frozen or canned fruit
sugar to taste
Crumble topping:
100g/4oz butter
175g/6oz plain flour
50g/2oz soft brown sugar
grated rind of ½ lemon

Place the fresh, defrosted or canned fruit in a heatproof dish and sprinkle with sugar to taste.

Rub the butter into the flour until the mixture resembles fine breadcrumbs. Stir in the sugar and lemon rind, blending well. Carefully spoon on top of the fruit and cook for 11–13 minutes, giving the dish a quarter-turn every 3 minutes. Brown under a preheated hot grill if liked. Serve hot with cream or custard.

Variations

Blackberry and apple crumble: Prepare as above using 225g/8 oz blackberries with 225g/8oz peeled, cored and sliced cooking apples.

Rhubarb and orange crumble: Prepare as above using 450g/1lb rhubarb chunks with the grated rind of 1 orange.

Berry crumble: Prepare as above, mixing equal quantities of redcurrants, blackcurrants and other berry fruits to make up to 450g/1lb.

St Clement's gooseberry crumble: Prepare as above but use 450g/1lb topped and tailed gooseberries with the grated rind of ½ orange and ½ lemon.

Baked Brazilian bananas

Serves: 4
Power setting: full
Total cooking time: 4 minutes

4 medium bananas
2 tablespoons lemon juice
2 tablespoons honey
50ml/2fl oz dry sherry, brown rum or orange juice
50g/2oz butter

Peel the bananas and place in a shallow dish. Brush with the lemon juice and spoon over the honey and sherry, rum or orange juice. Dot with the butter and cover loosely. Cook for 4 minutes, giving the dish a half-turn half-way during the cooking time. Serve hot with cream if liked.

Baked stuffed apples

Serves: 4
Power setting: full
Total cooking time: 9–10 minutes

4 large dessert or cooking apples
8 fresh or dried dates
4 tablespoons brown sugar
1 tablespoon butter
8 tablespoons water

Wash and remove the cores from the apples. With a sharp knife, cut a slit around the middle of each apple to prevent the skin from bursting during cooking. Stand upright in a shallow dish and stuff the centre of each apple with two of the dates. Sprinkle the tops with the sugar and dot with the butter. Pour the water around the fruit, cover and cook for 9–10 minutes until tender but not fallen.

Serve hot with custard or pouring cream.

Hot plum and orange compote

Serves: 4
Power setting: full
Total cooking time: 6½ minutes

25g/1oz seedless raisins
100ml/4fl oz medium dry sherry
3 tablespoons dark brown sugar
1 large orange
1 cinnamon stick
450g/1lb red plums, halved and stoned

Place the raisins in a small jug with the sherry, sugar, a large strip of finely pared orange rind and the cinnamon stick. Cover and cook for 2 minutes. Allow to cool.

When cool, remove and discard the orange rind and cinnamon stick. Place the plums in a dish and pour over the raisin mixture. Cover and cook for 4 minutes.

Meanwhile, peel the orange, remove the pith and slice into segments. Add to the hot plum mixture and cook, covered, for a further ½ minute.

Serve hot with soured cream or pouring cream.

Christmas pudding

Serves: 4–6
Power setting: full
Total cooking time: 8 minutes

75g/3oz fresh white breadcrumbs
75g/3oz plain flour
pinch of ground mace
pinch of ground nutmeg
pinch of ground ginger
pinch of ground cinnamon
75g/3oz shredded suet
50g/2oz soft brown sugar
50g/2oz castor sugar
50g/2oz chopped candied peel
75g/3oz currants
50g/2oz sultanas
150g/5oz raisins
40g/1½oz blanched almonds, chopped
1 small cooking apple, peeled, cored and chopped
grated rind and juice of ½ lemon
1 tablespoon brandy
1 large egg, beaten
3 tablespoons brown ale or stout
1 tablespoon milk
1½ tablespoons black treacle

In a large mixing bowl mix together all the dry ingredients, the almonds, apple and lemon rind. Mix the brandy with the egg, brown ale or stout, milk and treacle. Add to the dry ingredients to give a mixture with a soft dropping consistency. Cover and leave overnight or for 6–8 hours.

Turn into a greased 1.15l/2pint pudding basin. Cover loosely with cling film and cook for 8 minutes. Leave to stand for 5 minutes before turning out and serving with custard, cream or brandy butter.

Variation

Christmas pudding ring: To make a Christmas pudding to serve 8 or more it is advisable to cook the pudding mixture in a large ring mould since the traditional pudding shape is difficult to cook right through to the middle. Fill a 2.25l/4 pint baking ring mould with double the mixture above, cover loosely with cling film then cook for 15–18 minutes. Leave to stand for 5 minutes before turning out and serving as above. *Total cooking time*: 15–18 minutes.

Pears in red wine

Serves: 4
Power setting: full
Total cooking time: 10 minutes

250ml/8fl oz dry red wine
225g/8oz sugar
1 cinnamon stick
4 firm dessert pears

Place the wine, sugar and cinnamon stick in a bowl and cook for 2 minutes or until the sugar is dissolved.

Peel the pears, keeping the stalks intact, and stand them upright in the dish. Baste the fruit evenly with the red wine syrup.

Cover loosely with cling film or greaseproof paper and cook for 8 minutes, giving the dish a quarter-turn every 2 minutes. Allow to stand for 2 minutes then test with a fine skewer. The pears should be tender after standing. If not, cook for a further 1–2 minutes. Serve hot or chilled with pouring cream.

Granny's suet pudding with hot orange sauce

Serves: 4–6
Power setting: full
Total cooking time: 7½–9 minutes

Pudding:
75g/3oz self-raising flour
75g/3oz fresh white breadcrumbs
pinch of salt
75g/3oz shredded beef suet
50g/2oz castor sugar
1 egg, beaten
6 tablespoons milk

Sauce:
150ml/¼ pint orange curd
150ml/¼ pint water
1 tablespoon cornflour

Grease a 900ml/1½ pint pudding basin well or line it with cling film.

Mix the flour with the breadcrumbs, salt, suet and sugar, blending well. Add the egg and milk and mix to make a batter with a soft dropping consistency. Spoon into the prepared basin, cover with cling film and snip two holes in the top to allow the steam to escape. Cook for 4–5 minutes or until the pudding rises to the top of the basin.

Remove the cling film carefully and invert the pudding on to a serving plate.

Meanwhile, place the orange curd and half of the water in a large jug. Cook for 2 minutes until hot. Blend the cornflour with the remaining water and stir into the orange sauce, blending well. Cook for 2–3 minutes, stirring every minute.

Serve the suet pudding cut into wedges, with the hot orange sauce.

Flambéed baked fruits

Serves: 6
Power setting: full
Total cooking time: 6½–8½ minutes

450g/1lb stoned cherries, fresh or canned
450g/1lb plums, halved and stoned
225g/8oz blackberries, hulled
2 apples, cored and sliced
2 pears, cored and sliced
50g/2oz clear honey
5 tablespoons brandy
whipped cream to serve

Place the fruits and honey in a large heatproof serving bowl. Cover with cling film, snipping two holes in the top to allow the steam to escape. Cook for 6–8 minutes, stirring half-way through the cooking time. Remove the cling film.

Place the brandy in a small jug and cook for ½ minute. Pour into a ladle and ignite. Pour over the warm fruit and serve, at once, with whipped cream.

Jam suet pudding

Serves: 4–6
Power setting: full
Total cooking time: 4½–5 minutes

100g/4oz self-raising flour
50g/2oz shredded suet
50g/2oz castor sugar
1 teaspoon vanilla essence
1 egg, beaten
100ml/4fl oz milk
3 tablespoons jam

Grease a 1.15l/2 pint pudding basin well or line it with cling film.

Mix the flour with the suet and sugar and, using a fork, gradually add the vanilla essence, egg and milk, blending well to make a soft batter.

Place the jam in the base of the prepared basin and carefully spoon over the suet mixture. Cover with cling film, snipping two holes in the top to aid the escape of steam. Cook for 4½–5 minutes or until the pudding rises to the top of the basin.

Remove the cling film carefully and invert the pudding on to a serving plate. Cut into wedges and serve with a sweet sauce or custard.

Variation

Syrup suet pudding: Prepare as above but use 3 tablespoons of golden syrup instead of the jam.

Creamy rice pudding

Serves: 3–4
Power setting: full and defrost
Total cooking time: 35 minutes

50g/2oz pudding or round-grain rice
450ml/¾ pint boiling water
large pinch of ground nutmeg
strip of lemon rind

25g/1oz sugar
1 170g/6oz can evaporated milk
1 teaspoon butter
150ml/¼ pint double cream, whipped

Place the rice, water, nutmeg and lemon rind in a large deep dish, cover and cook on full power for 10 minutes, stirring half-way through the cooking time.

Remove and discard the lemon rind, stir in the sugar and evaporated milk, blending well. Cover and cook on defrost power for 20 minutes, stirring every 5 minutes.

Stir in the butter and cook on defrost power for a further 5 minutes. Allow to stand for 5 minutes then fold in the whipped cream. Serve warm or cold.

Baked citrus cheesecake

Serves: 6
Power setting: full
Total cooking time: 5½ minutes

Base:
75g/3oz butter
175g/6 oz digestive biscuits, crushed
Filling:
175g/6oz cream cheese
2 eggs, lightly beaten
pinch of salt
75g/3oz sugar
2 tablespoons frozen concentrated orange juice, thawed
1 tablespoon lemon juice
100ml/4fl oz soured cream
To decorate:
150 ml/¼ pint double cream, whipped
orange segments

Place the butter in a bowl and cook for 1½ minutes to melt. Stir in the biscuit crumbs, blending well. Press into a 20cm/8in china flan dish, lining the base and sides evenly.

Lightly whisk the filling ingredients together until smooth and carefully pour into the flan dish. Cook for 2 minutes, giving the dish a quarter-turn half-way through the cooking time. Cook for a further minute, giving the dish a quarter-turn half-way through the cooking time. Allow to stand for 1 minute then cook for a further minute. Allow to cool then chill thoroughly.

To serve, decorate the cheesecake with swirls of whipped cream and orange segments.

Greengage fool

Serves: 4
Power setting: full
Total cooking time: 8–10 minutes

900g/2lb greengages
2 tablespoons water
2 tablespoons clear honey
2 tablespoons castor sugar
300ml/½ pint custard (see page 127)
150ml/¼ pint double cream, whipped
To decorate:
chopped mixed nuts
mint sprigs

Stone and wash the greengages and place in a bowl with the water, honey and sugar. Cover with cling film, snipping two holes in the top to allow the steam to escape. Cook for 8–10 minutes until soft and pulpy. Allow to cool then purée in a liquidizer or pass through a fine sieve.

When the greengage purée is cold, whip the custard and fold it in with the double cream. Spoon into individual serving dishes and chill thoroughly.

Serve chilled, decorated with chopped nuts and mint sprigs.

Honey and mango mousse

Serves: 4
Power setting: full
Total cooking time: ½–1 minute

2 large ripe mangoes, peeled and stoned

15g/½oz powdered gelatine
1 tablespoon lemon juice
2 tablespoons water
2 tablespoons clear honey
150ml/¼ pint double cream
2 egg whites
mint sprigs to decorate (optional)

Purée the mango flesh in a blender or pass through a fine sieve.

Mix the gelatine with the lemon juice and water in a small jug and leave until the liquid is absorbed. Cook for ½–1 minute to dissolve the gelatine. Allow to cool slightly.

Stir the dissolved gelatine with the honey into the mango purée, blending well. Whip the cream until it stands in soft peaks and fold into the mango purée.

Whisk the egg whites until they stand in firm peaks. Fold into the mango mixture with a metal spoon. Divide equally between four soufflé or glass dessert dishes and chill until set.

Serve decorated with mint sprigs if liked.

Speedy lemon cheesecake

Serves: 4–6
Power setting: full
Total cooking time: 1½ minutes

Base:
50g/2oz butter
8 large digestive biscuits, crushed
25g/1oz demerara sugar
Topping:
3 eggs, separated
75g/3oz castor sugar
6 tablespoons lemon juice
15g/½oz powdered gelatine
2 tablespoons water
225g/8oz cream cheese
225g/8oz cottage cheese, sieved
150ml/¼ pint soured cream
To decorate:
2 oranges, peeled, pith removed and cut into segments

Place the butter in a bowl and cook for ½ minute to melt. Stir in the biscuit crumbs and sugar, blending well. Press into the base of a 20cm/8in spring form pan or flan tin. Chill to set.

Meanwhile, whisk the egg yolks with the sugar until very thick and mousse-like. Place the lemon juice, gelatine and water in a bowl, blending well. Cook for 1 minute to dissolve the gelatine. Allow to cool slightly.

Add the gelatine mixture, cream cheese, cottage cheese and soured cream to the egg mixture, blending well.

Whisk the egg whites until they stand in stiff peaks. Fold into the cheesecake mixture with a metal spoon. Pour over the chilled base and chill to set.

To serve, remove the cheesecake from the flan tin on to a serving dish and decorate with the orange segments. Cut into wedges to serve.

Basic vanilla ice cream

Serves: 4
Power setting: full
Total cooking time: 6 minutes

2 eggs, beaten
450ml/¾ pint milk
175g/6oz sugar
1 tablespoon vanilla essence
300ml/½ pint double cream

Mix the eggs, milk and sugar in a medium-sized bowl and cook for 6 minutes, stirring every 2 minutes until lightly thickened. Allow to cool then add the vanilla essence and cream, blending well.

Pour into a freezing tray and freeze until almost solid. Remove, allow to stand for 15–30 minutes, then whisk until smooth. Return to the freezer and freeze until firm.

Place in the refrigerator for about ½–1 hour to soften slightly before serving. Serve scooped into individual dishes or glasses.

Variations

Coffee ice cream: Dissolve 1 tablespoon instant coffee powder in 2 tablespoons of the double cream and 1 tablespoon brown rum (optional). Add with the double cream.

Raspberry ice cream: Purée 225g/8oz fresh or frozen raspberries to give 150ml/¼ pint purée. Add with the double cream.

Walnut and honey ice cream: Finely chop 50g/2oz walnuts and add to the double cream with 3 tablespoons set honey.

Strawberry ice cream: Purée 225g/8oz fresh or frozen strawberries to give 150ml/¼ pint purée. Add with the double cream.

Mocha ice cream: Melt 50g/2oz plain chocolate by cooking for ½ minute. Add with 1 tablespoon instant coffee to the double cream. *Total cooking time*: 6½ minutes.

Chestnut ice cream: Add 225g/8oz fresh or canned chestnut purée with the double cream.

Berry ice cream: Cook 225g/8oz berry fruits with a little sugar until the juice runs, about 2–3 minutes. Purée until smooth and sieve. Cool then add to the double cream. *Total cooking time*: 8–9 minutes.

Breads, cakes and biscuits

Basic white bread

Makes: 1kg/2lb loaf
Power setting: full or low
Total cooking time: 5½ or 8½–10½ minutes

1 teaspoon sugar
1 teaspoon dried yeast
300ml/½ pint warm water
450g/1lb plain flour
½ teaspoon salt
40g/1½oz butter or margarine
2 teaspoons oil
1 tablespoon poppy seeds or cracked wheat

Mix the sugar with the yeast and half of the water. Leave to stand in a warm place for 10 minutes until frothy.

Sift the flour and salt into a mixing bowl and cook on full power for ½ minute or until warm. Rub in the butter or margarine, add the yeast liquid and remaining water, and mix to a pliable dough. Knead on a lightly-floured surface until smooth and elastic – about 5 minutes. Return the dough to the bowl and cover with cling flm. Leave in a warm place until doubled in size. This proving can be hastened by using the microwave – simply cook for 5 seconds occasionally.

Knead the dough for a further 2–3 minutes then shape and place in either a 1kg/2lb glass loaf dish or a greased 15cm/6in soufflé dish. Leave in a warm place until doubled in size. The hastening process can be used again if liked.

Lightly brush the bread with oil and sprinkle with the poppy seeds or cracked wheat. Cook on full power for 5 minutes, giving the dish a half-turn twice during the cooking time or cook on full power for 1 minute, then on low power for 7–9 minutes, giving the dish a half-turn three times during the cooking time. Leave to stand for 5 minutes before turning out to cool on a wire rack. If a brown crust is liked then brown quickly under a preheated hot grill for a few minutes.

Variation

White bread rolls: Prepare and knead the dough and allow it to rise once, as above, but shape into 16 small rolls. Prove until doubled in size, then cook in two batches on a greased microwave baking tray, or on a piece of greased greaseproof paper, on full power for 2 minutes, re-arranging half-way through the cooking time. Cook the second batch in the same way. If a brown crust is liked, place the rolls under a hot grill for a few minutes. *Total cooking time*: 4½ minutes.

Farmhouse soda bread

Serves: 4
Power setting: medium and full
Total cooking time: 8 minutes

450g/1lb wholemeal flour
2 teaspoons bicarbonate of soda
2 teaspoons cream of tartar
1 teaspoon salt
25g/1oz lard
2 teaspoons castor sugar
300ml/½ pint milk
1 tablespoon lemon juice
25g/1oz porridge oats

Mix the flour with the bicarbonate of soda, cream of tartar and salt. Rub in the lard until the mixture resembles fine breadcrumbs then stir in the sugar. Mix the milk with the lemon juice and mix into the dry ingredients, blending well to make a soft dough. Knead on a lightly-floured surface until smooth and elastic then shape into a round. Place on a plate or microwave baking tray and mark into four sections with a sharp knife. Cook on medium power for 5 minutes, giving the dish a half-turn after 3 minutes.

Cook on full power for a further 3 minutes. Leave to stand for 10 minutes before transferring to a wire rack to cool.

Garlic and herb bread

Serves: 4–6
Power setting: full
Total cooking time: 1½ minutes

1 short, crusty French stick

100g/4oz butter
2 cloves garlic, peeled and crushed
2 teaspoons chopped fresh herbs

With a sharp knife, cut the stick into 2.5cm/1in slices, almost through to the base. Mix the butter with the garlic and herbs, blending well. Spread evenly between the slices of bread and re-form the loaf into a neat shape. Protect or shield the thin ends of the stick with small pieces of foil and cover the whole stick with dampened greaseproof paper.

Cook for 1½ minutes or until the butter has just melted and the bread is warm. Pull the slices apart to serve.

Honey and hazelnut tea cakes

Makes: 6
Power setting: full
Total cooking time: 6½ minutes

225g/8oz plain flour
pinch of salt
25g/1oz butter or margarine
1 teaspoon sugar
150ml/¼ pint milk
15g/½oz dried yeast
50g/2oz set honey
50g/2oz hazelnuts, roasted, skinned and chopped
50g/2oz chopped candied peel

Sift the flour and salt into a bowl. Rub in the butter or margarine until the mixture resembles fine breadcrumbs.

Meanwhile, add the sugar to the milk and cook for ½ minute. Stir in the yeast, blending well, and leave to stand for about 10–15 minutes or until frothy. Stir in the honey, blending well.

Mix the hazelnuts and candied peel with the flour. Add the yeast mixture and mix to a soft dough. Knead lightly, on a lightly floured surface, until smooth and elastic. Place in a greased bowl and cover with cling film. Prove the dough by heating for ¼ minute and leaving to stand for 5–10 minutes. Repeat this 3–4 times until the dough has doubled in size.

Knead again until the dough is smooth and elastic. Divide into six equal pieces and shape into flat rounds. Prove again as before until doubled in size.

Place half of the teacakes on a greased microwave baking tray or large plate. Cook, in two batches of three teacakes, for 2 minutes, re-arranging, if necessary, half-way through the cooking time. Allow to cool on a wire rack.

If a brown crust is liked, place the teacakes under a hot grill for a few minutes until golden. Serve split and buttered.

Genoese sponge

Serves: 6–8
Power setting: full
Total cooking time: 5½–6½ minutes

4 eggs
100g/4oz castor sugar
100g/4oz plain flour
pinch of salt
50g/2oz butter
5 tablespoons jam
150ml/¼ pint whipped cream
icing sugar to dust

Line a 320cm/8in cake dish or soufflé dish with cling film. Whisk the eggs and sugar together until they are pale and fluffy and have trebled in volume. Sift the flour and salt together and carefully sprinkle over the egg mixture. Meanwhile, place the butter in a bowl and cook for 1–1½ minutes to melt. Pour the butter over the egg and flour mixture in a steady stream. Gently fold the mixture to combine all the ingredients.

Pour into the prepared dish and cook for 4½–5 minutes, giving the dish a quarter-turn every 1½–2 minutes. Leave to stand for 5–10 minutes before turning out on to a wire rack to cool.

To serve, split the cake horizontally and sandwich together with the jam and cream. Dust the top with icing sugar. Cut into wedges to serve.

Victoria sandwich

Serves: 6–8
Power setting: full
Total cooking time: 6½–7½ minutes

175g/6oz butter or margarine
175g/6oz castor sugar
3 eggs, beaten
175g/6oz plain flour
2 teaspoons baking powder
pinch of salt
2 tablespoons hot water
5 tablespoons raspberry jam
icing sugar to dust

Line a 20cm/8in deep cake dish or soufflé dish with cling film, or lightly grease and line the base of the dish with greaseproof paper. Do not flour the sides of the dish.

Cream the butter and sugar until light and fluffy. Add the eggs, a little at a time, beating well to blend. Sift the flour with the baking powder and salt and fold into the creamed mixture with the hot water. Spoon into the prepared dish and level the surface carefully. Cook for 6½–7½ minutes, giving the dish a half-turn every 2 minutes. The cake will still be slightly sticky and moist on top when cooked – this will dry out and continue to cook with the residual heat in the cake. To test if cooked, insert a wooden cocktail stick into the cake; the cake is cooked if the stick comes out clean. Allow to stand in the dish for 5 minutes before turning out on to a wire rack to cool.

To serve, split the cake in half horizontally and sandwich together with the jam. Dust the top wth icing sugar. Cut into wedges to serve.

Variations

Victoria cream sandwich: Prepare as above but sandwich together with 2–3 tablespoons jam and 3–4 tablespoons whipped cream.

Victoria walnut sandwich: Prepare as above but fold 25g/1oz very finely chopped walnuts into the creamed mixture after beating in the eggs.

Victoria citrus sandwich: Prepare as above but cream the sugar and butter with 1 teaspoon each of finely grated lemon and orange rind.

Dutch apple and lemon cake

Serves: 6
Power setting: medium/high
Total cooking time: 11–11½ minutes

175g/6oz butter
100g/4oz castor sugar
3 eggs, beaten
2 tablespoons golden syrup
juice and finely grated rind of 1 lemon
200g/7oz self-raising flour
50g/2oz walnuts, chopped
1 small eating apple, peeled, cored and chopped
Lemon icing:
2 tablespoons milk
50g/2oz butter
200g/7oz icing sugar, sifted
juice of ½ lemon
To decorate:
halved walnuts

Line a 1.2l/2pint cake dish or soufflé dish with cling film. Cream the butter and sugar until light and fluffy. Add the eggs, a little at a time, beating well to blend. Add the golden syrup, lemon juice and rind. Fold in the flour, walnuts and apple. Spoon into the prepared dish and cook for 10½–11 minutes, giving the dish a quarter-turn every 2½ minutes. When cooked the top of the cake will still appear wet – this will cook with the residual heat in the cake when removed from the oven. Leave to stand for 10 minutes then turn out on to a wire rack to cool.

To make the icing, place the milk and butter in a bowl and cook for ½ minute. Beat in the icing sugar and lemon juice. If the mixture appears a little dry, cook for a further ½ minute. Spread on top of the cake at once. Decorate with halved walnuts. Cut into wedges to serve.

Golden chocolate cake

Serves: 6
Power setting: full
Total cooking time: 7½–8 minutes

100g/4oz butter
100g/4oz castor sugar
2 eggs
100g/4oz self-raising flour
50g/2oz cocoa powder
40g/1½ oz ground almonds
100ml/4fl oz milk
4 tablespoons golden syrup
Chocolate icing:
2 tablespoons milk
50g/2oz butter
1 tablespoon cocoa powder
200g/7oz icing sugar, sifted
To decorate:
chocolate curls

Line a 1.2l/2 pint cake dish or soufflé dish with cling film. Cream the butter and sugar together until light and fluffy. Beat in the eggs, one at a time. Carefully fold in the flour, cocoa powder and ground almonds. Add the milk and golden syrup, mixing well to blend. Spoon into the prepared dish and cook for 6½–7 minutes, giving the dish a quarter-turn every 1½ minutes. When cooked the top of the cake will still appear wet – this will cook with the residual heat in the cake when removed from the oven. Leave to stand for 10 minutes then turn out on to a wire rack to cool.

To make the icing, place the milk, butter and cocoa powder in a bowl and cook for 1 minute. Beat in the icing sugar until smooth. If the mixture appears a little dry, cook for a further ½ minute. Spread on top of the cake at once. Decorate with chocolate curls. Cut into wedges to serve.

Blackcurrant cheesecake

Serves: 6–8
Power setting: full

Total cooking time: 2–2½ minutes

Base:
75g/3oz butter
1 150g/5.3oz packet Nice biscuits, crushed
Filling:
175g/6oz full-fat soft cream cheese
50g/2oz castor sugar
2 eggs, separated
15g/½oz powdered gelatine
3 tablespoons blackcurrant health drink
1 150g/5.3oz carton blackcurrant yoghurt
150ml/¼ pint whipping cream
To decorate:
whipped cream
hazelnuts

Grease the base and sides of a 20cm/8in spring release cake tin and line with greaseproof paper.

Place the butter in a bowl and cook for 1–2 minutes to melt. Mix with the biscuit crumbs, blending well to coat. Press into the base of the tin and chill to set.

Meanwhile, beat the cheese and sugar together until soft and creamy. Add the egg yolks and beat until smooth. Mix the gelatine with the blackcurrant health drink and leave until the liquid is absorbed. Cook for ½ minute to dissolve the gelatine. Stir into the cheese mixture, blending well. Whisk in the yoghurt then leave until just beginning to set around the edges.

Whip the cream until it stands in soft peaks and fold into the blackcurrant mixture. Whisk the egg whites until stiff and fold into the cheesecake mixture, blending well. Quickly pour on to the biscuit crust and chill until set.

To serve, remove from the tin and carefully peel off the greaseproof paper. Decorate with swirls of whipped cream and hazelnuts.

Apricot tart

Serves: 6–8
Power setting: full
Total cooking time: 5–6½ minutes

Pastry:

125g/4oz plain flour

pinch of salt

75g/3oz unsalted butter

1½ tablespoons castor sugar

about 2 teaspoons water

Filling:

175g/6oz full-fat cream cheese

3 tablespoons set or creamed honey

½ teaspoon ground cinnamon

Topping:

450g/1lb fresh apricots, halved and stoned or 1 420g/14.8oz can apricot halves, drained

2–3 tablespoons clear honey

1 tablespoon toasted almond flakes

Sift the flour with the salt into a bowl. Rub in the butter until the mixture resembles fine breadcrumbs. Stir in the sugar and sufficient water to bind to a firm but pliable dough Roll out the pastry on a lightly floured surface to a round large enough to line a 20cm/8in flan dish. Press in firmly taking care not to stretch the pastry. Cut the pastry away leaving a 5mm/¼in 'collar' above the dish (this allows for any shrinkage that may occur). Prick the base well with a fork. Line the inside, upright edge of the pastry case with a long strip of foil, about 4cm/1½in wide (this prevents the outer edges from over-cooking). Place a double thickness layer of absorbent kitchen towel over the base, easing into position around the edges to keep the foil in place. Cook for 4–4½ minutes, giving the dish a quarter-turn every minute. Remove the paper and foil and cook for a further 1–2 minutes. Allow to cool.

To make the filling, beat the cream cheese with the honey and cinnamon, blending well. Spread over the base of the pastry case. Chill until required.

Just before serving arrange the apricot halves on top of the filling and brush with the clear honey. Sprinkle with toasted almonds and serve at once. Cut into wedges to serve.

Mincemeat tartlets Noel

Makes: about 16

Power setting: full
Total cooking time: 19–24 minutes

225g/8oz shortcrust pastry
flour to dust
275g/10oz mincemeat
Brandy butter:
75g/3 oz butter
175g/6oz icing sugar
3–4 tablespoons brandy
grated lemon and orange peel

Roll out the pastry on a lightly-floured surface until thin. Using a fluted cutter, cut into small circles, large enough to cover the bases of ramekins, teacups or other small dishs. Place a piece of greaseproof paper over the base of each inverted container, then mould the rolled-out pastry rounds over the top. To cook, arrange in a circle on the base of the microwave, four at a time, and cook for 4–5 minutes. Allow to stand for 5 minutes before carefully removing the pastry from the dishes.

Place the mincemeat in a bowl and cook until bubbly and hot, about 3–4 minutes. Spoon equal amounts of the mixture into the cooked tartlet cases. Allow to cool.

Meanwhile, cream the butter until pale and soft then gradually add the icing sugar, beating to keep smooth. Finally beat in the brandy.

When the mincemeat tartlets are cool top each with a swirl of brandy butter and sprinkle with orange or lemon peel.

Lemon shortbread

Makes: 8 pieces
Power setting: full
Total cooking time: 3–4 minutes

175g/6 oz plain flour
50g/2oz ground rice
pinch of salt
finely grated rind of 1 lemon
150g/5oz butter, softened
50g/2oz castor sugar

Line an 18cm/7in fluted ceramic flan dish with cling film. Sift the flour, ground rice and salt into a bowl and mix with the lemon rind. Rub in the butter until the mixture resembles fine breadcrumbs. Stir in half of the sugar and knead together lightly to form a dough.

Press the lemon shortbread mixture into the flan dish with the back of a spoon. Mark into 8 wedges with a sharp knife and prick well. Flute the edges of the shortbread if liked by pinching with the fingers. Cook for 3–4 minutes, giving the dish a quarter-turn every minute. Sprinkle with the remaining sugar and allow to cool slightly. Cut into wedges, turn out, and allow to cool completely on a wire rack.

Anzac biscuits

Makes: about 50
Power setting: full
Total cooking time: 8–9 minutes

100g/4oz butter
1 tablespoon golden syrup
1 teaspoon bicarbonate of soda
2 tablespoons boiling water
100g/4oz rolled oats
175g/6oz desiccated coconut
100g/4oz plain flour
225g/8oz sugar

Place the butter and golden syrup in a bowl and cook for 2 minutes. Blend the bicarbonate of soda with the water and stir into the butter mixture. Mix the remaining ingredients together in a mixing bowl and pour the melted mixture over. Mix well to combine to a moist but stiff mixture.

Lightly grease a microwave baking sheet and drop teaspoons of the mixture on to it about 4cm/1½in apart (the biscuits will generally have to be cooked in two batches). Cook for 3–3½ minutes, giving the dish a half-turn after 2 minutes. Allow to cool until firm enough to lift then transfer to a wire rack to cool. Repeat with the remaining mixture.

Drinks

Guide to heating coffee and milk

	Time in minutes on full power
Black coffee	
600ml/1 pint (cold)	4½–5
1.15l/2 pints (cold)	7–7½
Milk	
150ml/1¼ pint (cold)	1–1½
300ml/½ pint (cold)	2–2½
Coffee and milk together	
600ml/1 pint coffee and 150ml/¼ pint milk (both cold)	5–5½
1.15l/2 pints coffee and 300ml/½ pint milk (both cold)	8–8½

Glühwein

Serves: 4
Power setting: full
Total cooking time: 4 minutes

600ml/1 pint dry or medium red wine
75g/3oz brown sugar
2 cinnamon sticks
1 lemon stuck with cloves
100ml/4 fl oz brandy

Place the wine, sugar, cinnamon sticks and lemon in a large heatproof jug or bowl and cook for 4 minutes or until boiling.

Addpoge brandy and leave to stand, covered, for 5 minutes. Strain and serve at once.

Irish coffee

Serves: 1
Power setting: full
Total cooking time: 1½–2 minutes

1 teaspoon sugar
150ml/¼ pint strong black coffee
2–3 tablespoons Irish whiskey
1–2 tablespoons double cream

Dissolve the sugar in the coffee in an Irish coffee or stemmed, heatproof glass. Cook, uncovered, for 1½–2 minutes or until very hot. Stir in the whiskey and carefully float the cream on top of the coffee mixture. Serve at once.

Variations

Jamaican or Caribbean coffee: Prepare as above but use rum instead of Irish whiskey.

Calypso coffee: Prepare as above but use Tia Maria instead of Irish whiskey.

French coffee: Prepare as above but use brandy instead of Irish whiskey.

German coffee: Prepare as above but use Kirsch instead of Irish whiskey.

Normandy coffee: Prepare as above but use Calvados instead of Irish whiskey.

Russian coffee: Prepare as above but use vodka instead of Irish whiskey.

Spanish coffee: Prepare as above but use sherry instead of Irish whiskey.

Cappuccino

Serves: 4
Power setting: full
Total cooking time: 3 minutes

450 ml/¾ pint milk
40g/1½ oz plain dessert chocolate, grated
4 teaspoons sugar
2 teaspoons instant coffee powder or granules
100ml/4fl oz brandy
Topping:
150 ml/¼ pint whipping cream, lightly whipped
chocolate curls to decorate

Place the milk in a large heatproof jug and cook for 3 minutes. Stir in the chocolate, sugar and coffee, blending well. Pour into individual heatproof glasses or mugs. Add 25ml/1fl oz of the brandy to each but do not stir. Top with a little whipped cream and decorate with chocolate curls.

Mulled cider

Serves: 4
Power setting: full
Total cooking time: 6 minutes

900 ml/1½ pints cider
50g/2oz brown sugar
1 cinnamon stick
3 whole cloves
To garnish:
orange slices

Place the cider in a large heatproof jug or bowl with the sugar, cinnamon and cloves. Cook for 6 minutes, stirring half-way through the cooking time. Leave to stand for 10 minutes then strain and serve hot, garnished with orange slices.

Old-fashioned cocoa

Serves: 4–6
Power setting: full
Total cooking time: 4–4½ minutes

50g/2oz sugar
8 teaspoons unsweetened cocoa powder
900ml/1½ pints milk

Mix the sugar with the cocoa powder in a large heatproof bowl or jug.
Mix with about 150ml/¼ pint of milk and cook for 1–1½ minutes or
until steaming hot.

   Add the remaining milk and cook for a further 3 minutes or until
piping hot but not boiling. Serve at once.

Preserves

Blackberry jam with Grand Marnier

Makes: about 1kg/2lb
Power setting: full
Total cooking time: 13–16 minutes

450g/1lb castor sugar
150ml/¼ pint hot water
675g/1½ lb blackberries, hulled
3 tablespoons Grand Marnier

Place the sugar and water in a large heatproof bowl and cook for 3 minutes or until the sugar has dissolved, stirring half-way through the cooking time. Add the blackberries and cook for 8–10 minutes, stirring half-way through the cooking time. Test for setting by placing a little of the jam on a cold saucer, leave for 1–2 minutes and if a skin forms on the surface and wrinkles when lightly pushed with the finger it is ready. When the jam is ready, stir in the Grand Marnier, mixing well. If a skin does not form then cook for a further 2–3 minutes and test again.

Ladle into warm sterilized jars, cover, seal and label. Store in a cool dark place until required.

Lemon curd

Makes: 675g/1½lb
Power setting: full and low
Total cooking time: 17–19 minutes

100g/4 oz butter
grated rind and juice of 3 lemons
225g/8 oz granulated sugar
3 eggs
1 egg yolk

Place the butter, lemon rind and juice in a large bowl and cook on full power for 3 minutes. Stir well to blend then add the sugar. Stir again and cook on full power for 2 minutes. Beat the eggs with the egg yolk and add to the mixture, blending well. Cook, uncovered, on low power for 12–14 minutes until the mixture is thickened and will coat the back of a wooden spoon. Stir occasionally to keep the lemon curd smooth.

Spoon into clean sterilized jars. Cover, seal, label and store in a cool place or the refrigerator until required. Keeps for 2–3 weeks.

Apple and mint jelly

Makes: about 1kg/2lb
Power setting: full
Total cooking time: 17–21 minutes

475ml/16 fl oz unsweetened apple juice
800g/1¾ lb granulated sugar
5 tablespoons commercial pectin
3 tablespoons chopped fresh mint
few drops of green food colouring (optional)

Place the apple juice and sugar in a large heatproof bowl, cover and cook for 12–14 minutes, stirring half-way through the cooking time.

Stir in the pectin, mixing well. Cover and cook for 4–6 minutes or until the mixture boils. Boil the mixture for 1 minute, stir, and remove any foam.

Stir in the chopped mint and colour with green food colouring if liked. Ladle into clean sterilized and warmed jars. Cover, seal, label and store in a cool place until required.

Dutch apple butter

Makes: about 1.5kg/3 lb
Power setting: full
Total cooking time: 20–26 minutes

900g/2lb cooking apples, peeled, cored and chopped
1 tablespoon water
225g/8oz set or clear honey
½ teaspoon ground cinnamon
¼ teaspoon ground nutmeg
¼ teaspoon ground cloves

Place the apples in a large heatproof dish with the water. Cover and cook for 12–16 minutes or until fallen and soft. Purée in a blender or pass through a fine sieve and return to the dish.

Stir in the honey and spices, blending well. Cook, uncovered, for

8–10 minutes, stirring occasionally, until buttery in texture. Ladle into warm sterilized jars, cover, seal and label. Store in a cool place for up to 2 weeks.

Dutch apple butter is served like jam with buns, toast and scones.

Microwave and convection cooking

Microwave and convection cooking

Convection cooking has been used by chefs and domestic cooks alike for many years; it has proved an ideal method for both roasting and baking. Hot air is circulated through the oven cavity by a high speed fan and this constant movement of heat surrounds the food, heats the outside and seals in the moisture and natural juices.

The introduction of convection to microwave cooking is new on the domestic scene but is likely to be a popular alternative to basic microwave cooking at the premium end of the market. Convection with microwave cooking speeds up the cooking time and allows a greater and more varied selection of dishes to be cooked. It also effectively solves the problem of browning – perhaps the major disadvantage of microwave cooking.

Most ovens available can be used for convection cooking alone, microwave alone, or a combination of convection and microwave which is very versatile. The recipes which follow in this section are for microwave and convection cooking combined.

Combination cooking gives baked and roasted dishes their usual brown appearance but it is important to follow manufacturer's instructions on preheating the convection oven – usually about 10 minutes. Convection to microwave cooking can then be done automatically or can be set manually – the choice is yours.

Roast potatoes

Serves: 2–3
Convection setting: 230°C
Power setting: full
Total cooking time: 32–35 minutes

450g/1lb potatoes, peeled and cut into pieces
4 tablespoons water
3 tablespoons oil, dripping or meat roasting fat

Place the potatoes in a bowl with the water. Cover with cling film, snipping two holes in the top to allow the steam to escape. Cook, on full power, for 12 minutes. Drain.

Place the oil, dripping or meat roasting fat in a roasting tin. Cook, on the convection rack, at 230°C, for 10 minutes.

Place the potatoes in the tin, turning and basting them with the hot fat. Cook, on the convection rack, at 230°C, for 20–25 minutes until golden and crisp. Turn the potatoes over half-way through the cooking time. Drain on absorbent kitchen towel and serve hot.

Savoury toad in the hole

Serves: 2–3
Convection setting: 230°C
Power setting: full
Total cooking time: 50 minutes (including preheating)

8 chipolata sausages
1 onion, peeled and thinly sliced
1 tablespoon oil
100g/4oz plain flour
pinch of salt
1 egg
300ml/½ pint milk or milk and water mixed
1 teaspoon dried mixed herbs

Preheat the oven to 230°C for 10 minutes. Place the sausages, onion and oil in a medium-sized dish. Cook, on the convection rack, for 10 minutes.

Meanwhile, sift the flour and salt into a bowl. Make a well in the centre and add the egg. Mix, gradually drawing the flour into the egg, to make a thick paste. Gradually add the milk or milk and water, beating well to make a smooth batter. Stir in the herbs, blending well.

Pour the prepared batter over the sausage mixture, return to the oven and cook, at 230°C, for 25 minutes, then on full power for 5 minutes. Serve hot.

Russian fish pie

Serves: 4
Convection setting: 230°C
Power setting: full
Total cooking time: 25–27 minutes

450g/1lb white fish fillets

600ml/1 pint Béchamel sauce (see page 122)
100g/4oz small button mushrooms
100g/4oz peeled prawns
salt and freshly ground white pepper
450g/1lb frozen puff pastry, thawed
beaten egg to glaze

Place the fish fillets in a shallow dish, cover with cling film, snipping two holes in the top to allow the steam to escape. Cook on full power for 5–7 minutes. Remove any skin and bones from the fish, and flake. Mix with the sauce, mushrooms, prawns, and salt and pepper to taste. Spoon into four individual pie dishes and leave to cool slightly while preparing the pastry lids.

Roll out the pastry on a lightly floured surface and cut into four rounds about 4cm/1½in larger than the pie dishes. Trim a 2.5cm/1in strip from each and use to line the dampened rims of each dish. Dampen the pastry rims with water and cover with the pastry lids. Trim, seal and flute the edges. Use any trimmings to decorate the pies as liked.

Brush with beaten egg to glaze and cook on the convection rack, at 230°C, for 20 minutes or until the pastry is well risen and golden brown.

Gougère with ham and mushrooms

Serves: 4
Convection setting: 210°C
Power setting: full
Total cooking time: 54–64½ minutes

Choux pastry:
150ml/¼ pint water
50g/2oz butter
65g/2½oz plain flour
pinch of salt
2 eggs, beaten
50g/2oz Cheddar cheese, grated
Filling:
25g/1oz butter
2 onions, peeled and sliced
50g/2oz button mushrooms, sliced

2 teaspoons plain flour
150ml/¼ pint chicken stock
3 tomatoes, peeled, seeded and quartered
100g/4 oz cooked ham, chopped
salt and freshly ground black pepper
1 tablespoon grated Parmesan cheese
1 tablespoon browned breadcrumbs
chopped parsley to garnish

Place the water and butter for the choux pastry in a bowl and cook on full power for 1½–2 minutes or until the butter has melted and the mixture boils. Add the flour and salt quickly and beat well to make a smooth paste. Cook, uncovered, for a further minute. Add the eggs and beat well to make a smooth shiny paste. Finally beat in the cheese, blending well.

Grease a medium-sized ovenproof dish and spoon or pipe the choux paste over the base and around the sides of the dish, leaving the centre hollow.

Meanwhile, prepare the filling. Place the butter in a bowl and cook on full power for ½ minute. Add the onion and cook for a further 5 minutes, stirring half-way through the cooking time. Add the mushrooms and cook for a further 3 minutes. Blend in the flour and stock and cook for a further 3 minutes. Add the tomatoes, ham and salt and pepper to taste, blending well. Preheat the convection oven to 210°C.

Spoon the prepared filling into the choux-lined dish and sprinkle with the Parmesan cheese and the breadcrumbs. Cook, on the convection rack, at 210°C, for 40–50 minutes. Sprinkle with parsley to garnish before serving.

Apple amber

Serves: 4
Convection setting: 230°C then 150°C
Power setting: full
Total cooking time: 31–43 minutes

175g/6oz prepared shortcrust pastry
Filling:
450g/1lb cooking apples, peeled, cored and sliced

50g/2oz butter
sugar to taste
grated rind of 1 lemon
juice of 1 lemon
2 large egg yolks, beaten
Meringue:
2 large egg whites
75g/3oz castor sugar

Roll out the prepared pastry on a lightly-floured surface and use to line a 20cm/8in flan tin.

Place the apples in a bowl with the butter. Cover and cook for 6–8 minutes, or until the apples are tender. Purée the mixture in a blender or pass through a fine seive. Sweeten with sugar to taste. Add the lemon rind, lemon juice and egg yolks, beating well to blend. Pour into the pastry-lined flan. Preheat the oven to 230°C.

Cook the flan, on the convection rack, for 15 minutes until the pastry is golden and the filling is set.

Meanwhile, whisk the egg whites until they stand in stiff peaks. Fold in 50g/2oz of the sugar with a metal spoon. Pile the meringue on top of the flan and sprinkle with the remaining sugar. Reduce the oven to 150°C.

Cook the flan for 10–20 minutes or until the meringue is a light golden colour and crisp to the touch.

Yorkshire tart

Serves: 4–6
Convection setting: 200°C
Power setting: medium
Total cooking time: 28 minutes

175g/6 oz prepared shortcrust pastry
3 tablespoons raspberry jam
75g/3oz butter
75g/3oz castor sugar
1 egg, beaten
75g/3oz plain flour
¼ teaspoon baking powder
25g/1oz ground almonds
finely grated rind of 1 lemon

milk to mix

Roll out the prepared pastry on a lightly-floured surface and use to line a 20cm/8in flan tin. Spread the jam over the pastry base. Preheat the oven to 200°C.

Cream the butter and sugar until light and fluffy. Beat in the egg, flour, ground almonds, lemon rind, and sufficient milk to make a mixture with a soft dropping consistency. Spread over the jam, levelling the surface.

Cook the tart, on the convection rack, for 25 minutes, then for 5 minutes on medium power. Allow to cool and serve warm or cut into wedges.

Christmas cake

Makes: 1 18cm/7in cake
Convection setting: 150°C
Power setting: medium
Total cooking time: 1¾ hours

100g/4oz butter
150g/5oz soft brown sugar
3 large eggs
1 tablespoon black treacle
175g/6 oz plain flour
¾ teaspoon ground mixed spice
¼ teaspoon ground nutmeg
40g/1½oz ground almonds
50g/2oz blanched almonds, chopped
225g/8oz currants
100g/4oz sultanas
100g/4oz raisins
50g/2oz glacé cherries, halved
50g/2oz mixed cut peel
1½ tablespoons brandy or sherry

Cream the butter and sugar until light and fluffy. Beat in the eggs with the treacle, blending well. Sift the flour with the spices and fold into the creamed mixture. Add the fruit, ground and blanched almonds, and the peel and mix well. Spoon into a greased and lined 18cm/7in round cake tin and level the surface. Preheat the oven to 150°C.

Cook the cake, on the convection rack, for 1 hour 40 minutes then on medium power for 5 minutes. Allow to cool in the tin for 5 minutes. While still slightly warm prick the base of the cake with a fine skewer. Pour the brandy or sherry over and allow to soak in. Allow to cook completely then wrap in foil and keep in an airtight tin until required.

Index